Japanese Kimonos of the 16th–20th Centuries

Robes of Elegance

Japanese Kimonos of the 16th–20th Centuries

Robes of Elegance

Ishimura Hayao and Maruyama Nobuhiko

with essays by

Yamanobe Tomoyuki

Published in conjunction with the exhibition organized by
the North Carolina Museum of Art
in association with
the National Museum of Japanese History, Sakura, assisted by
the National Museum of Modern Art, Tokyo.

North Carolina Museum of Art, Raleigh

Robes of Elegance: Japanese Kimonos of the 16th–20th Centuries

March 12–June 19, 1988
North Carolina Museum of Art

This exhibition and catalogue are supported by generous funding from American Airlines, the National Endowment for the Arts, a federal agency, and the North Carolina Museum of Art Foundation.

NOTE: Throughout the catalogue, all Japanese names are given in Japanese order, surname first.

The North Carolina Museum of Art is an agency of the State of North Carolina, James G. Martin, Governor, and of the Department of Cultural Resources, Patric Dorsey, Secretary.

Copyright 1988 North Carolina Museum of Art
Library of Congress Catalogue Number 87-62987
ISBN 0-88259-955-0

Translated by Haruko Ward
Designed by the North Carolina Museum of Art Design Department
Typeset in Sabon by Marathon Typography Service, Inc.
Printed by Dai Nippon Printing Co., Ltd., Tokyo

Photos courtesy National Museum of Japanese History, Sakura, and the National Museum of Modern Art, Tokyo.

Cover:
Screen with Two *Kosode*. Left: *Kosode* fragment with chrysanthemums and bamboo fence. Embroidery and *shibori* on figured satin. Mid-Edo period, late seventeenth century to early eighteenth century. Right: *Kosode* fragment with morning glories. *Shibori*, dyeing, and embroidery on crimson crepe. Late Edo period, nineteenth century.

Contents

vii	Foreword	Yamanobe Tomoyuki
ix	Introduction	Richard S. Schneiderman
xiii	Acknowledgments	Richard S. Schneiderman
1	The Nomura Collection	Maruyama Nobuhiko
3	*Kosode* of the Premodern Age	Maruyama Nobuhiko
20	*Kosode* at the End of the Premodern Age	Yamanobe Tomoyuki
23	*Yūzen* Dyeing	Maruyama Nobuhiko
33	The Modern Kimono	Ishimura Hayao
43	Chronology	
45	Catalogue	
	Entries 1-75	Maruyama Nobuhiko
	Entries 76-90	Ishimura Hayao
241	Glossary	
245	Diagram of a *Kosode*	

Foreword

The archetypal kimono is the *kosode*, whose history of decoration dates to the end of the fifteenth century. People's "dream" of decorating their *kosode* with beautiful, flexible, and colorful pictures inspired them to create and experiment with new techniques. During the Momoyama period (1573–1615), two techniques of decoration were established: *nuihaku*, a prevalent embroidery technique well suited to rendering pictorial designs with flexible shapes and colors, and *tsujigahana*, in which dyeing, delineation and shading in ink, *surihaku* (applied metallic leaf), and sometimes embroidery were used to execute the designs. The techniques and methods of producing *kosode* were explored to their fullest, and today's viewers can appreciate the creative spirit of the premodern *kosode*.

During the Edo period, *kosode* designs increased even further the parameters of pictorial expression. The basic techniques of this period were *shibori* (resist dyeing), embroidery, and partial *nurizome* (brush painting with dyes). The *nurizome* method gradually evolved into the *yūzen* dyeing technique. Another new technique, *surihitta*, which imitated the effects of *shibori*-style resist through the use of stencil patterns, also came into fashion around this time.

The representative style of *kosode* of the early half of the Edo period (mid-seventeenth century) was the Kanbun *kosode*. In this style a bold design was depicted in a diagonal flow from the right shoulder to the left skirt of the back of the *kosode*, resulting in a strong statement contrasting with the quiet, undecorated area of the left shoulder. This was an excellent design which required the viewer to exercise his imagination. The Kanbun-style *kosode* continued in popularity until the following Genroku years. After the wider *obi* sash came into fashion, the design elements spread over the entire surface of the kimono, losing the tension of the Kanbun design.

In the eighteenth century, *yūzen* dyeing, considered a virtual revolution in Japanese textile techniques, flourished. The major characteristic of this technique was *nurizome*, the application of pigmented dyes with paint brushes after paste resist had been completed. This technique made easier the rendering of any color and shape, and partial shading was possible as well. With *yūzen*, the pictorial possibilities were almost limitless, and the beauty of the *kosode* increased dramatically.

The basis of kimono decoration thus was established in the decoration of the premodern *kosode*. From then until the present time, with these basic applied design techniques, beautiful kimono designs have been created continuously. It should not be forgotten that such decorative *kosode* actually were worn daily. The designs were born from the imagination and experience of the upper and wealthy middle classes of the period. Despite their origin, or perhaps because of it, the designs of the kimono, or *kosode*, so popular hundreds of years ago, have great appeal to us even today.

I hope that you will learn about the Japanese designs which developed on the surface of the kimono and come to understand the rich and wonderful sense of decorative beauty enjoyed by the Japanese people.

Yamanobe Tomoyuki
Former Curator, Textiles Section
Tokyo National Museum

Introduction

One commentator has said that the kimono places a heavy responsibility, a burden, on its wearer. So great is the tradition of the kimono, the modern descendant of the *kosode*, that there is no Western garment that is comparable to it. For the Japanese people, this robe has the formality of evening attire, the creativity and prestige of a designer original, and the tradition of Scottish kilts, academic regalia, or wedding gowns. However, the *kosode* was at times in Japanese history almost universal apparel. Even today they are not reserved just for ceremonial or festive occasions; in fact it is not uncommon to see Japanese women doing their shopping in kimonos.

To fully appreciate the feeling of tradition and reverence that Japanese people hold for the kimono, the Westerner must understand something of Japanese thinking. Wearing kimonos is not simply the acceptance of tradition, because for many Japanese people there is no question of not accepting one's tradition and responsibilities, but more an expression of a feeling of indebtedness to the circumstances of one's life. Perhaps there is no more visible symbol of the acceptance of tradition and responsibility than the wearing of kimonos. When the kimono is put on, the wearer is tied to more than nine centuries of Japanese culture, history, and protocol.

The development and final adoption of the *kosode* is related not only to the development of native Japanese domestic architecture but also to leisure activities. Like steppingstones which meander through a garden to invite leisurely, but controlled, walking and to stimulate contemplation of nature's beauty, the *kosode*, impractical for work or hurried activity, was eminently suitable for thoughtful strolling or for the wearer to sit on his knees. Although all classes wore *kosode* as a principal outer garment by the end of the fifteenth century, it must be acknowledged that such highly decorated robes as those in this exhibition were reserved for the court and attendants, people at leisure, or special occasions.

The basic *kosode* has remained relatively unchanged since the late Heian period (794-1185). Materials as well as design and dyeing techniques have changed, but not as radically as one might expect. Some of the boldest patterns, seemingly so modern, date to the late seventeenth century, such as the *kosode* with frames (No. 11) or *kosode* with scattered flutes (No. 12). Such boldness of design was a result of the exuberance of the long period of peace under the Tokugawa shoguns, which followed a century and a half of almost continual warfare. The rise of a growing class of townsmen, comprising wealthy merchants, entertainers, and artisans, who produced goods desired by the affluent, created a demand for luxury items above and beyond that required by the shogun and court. Considered the lowest order of the Japanese social hierarchy, and perhaps because of that, these townsmen broke from the traditions of the court and military elite to establish a style of their own.

Fashion was stimulated by the kabuki theater, which was considered outrageously vulgar by the samurai class. Although an affront to refined sensibilities, the kabuki theater became the very center of social life. Performances lasted all day and the auditorium was packed, often with housewives who emulated kabuki costumes, hairstyles, and mannerisms. However, the taste for bold patterns such as stripes and checks extended the vocabulary of design for the seventeenth-century *kosode*. In an attempt to stem what was considered to be a tide of extravagance in the late seventeenth century, the shogunate passed laws that controlled what people could wear, thus controlling creative and innovative design. The elaborate *kosode* came to be worn only for ceremonial and festive occasions. The period following the extravagance of the late seventeenth century until the Meiji Restoration (1868-1912) was a period of restored elegance, with emphasis placed on muted colors and elaborate but barely visible woven patterns. Decorative embroidery and dyeing were often restricted to the interior lining of the *kosode*.

The opening of Japan during the latter part of the nineteenth century carried with it the Westernization of some aspects of Japanese culture. The adoption of Western-style clothing approached such universal acceptance that the empress Teimei issued a decree in 1912 that kimonos would be worn at official and ceremonial occasions. Sparking a renaissance in traditional garments, artists again turned their attention to *kosode*, which took on new significance as an art form unique to Japan.

During the course of the research for this exhibition, this author interviewed several kimono artists. Some common themes emerged from these discussions that shed light on the art form today. There is a strong sense among the artists of the tradition of the art. It was said that success is to reach or strive for the level of achievement attained by their predecessors, which presents many of these artists with an exceptional challenge. Several times, the artists spoke of the "transference of heritage," or the need to transfer the tradition to future generations. This mantle of responsibility demands a purity and beauty, not only of expression, but of thought and personal aesthetic philosophy, which must challenge future generations.

Another common thread that binds these artists together is the desire to create art, in the form of kimonos, that reflects their own aesthetic, not for the sake of change or for the expression of an individual's creativity, but as an end of the learning process. An artist respects what has been done in the past, but one cannot repeat past achievements. In the same vein, the process of learning necessarily involves going beyond what has been done before. Specifically, in weaving it was said that to learn technique the artist must change patterns. To be as good as those of the past, an artist must be better than those before him.

Today in Japan, kimonos are worn in everyday situations, for ceremony and festivals, and they are sought after and prized by collectors. One of the first to recognize and collect Japanese kimonos was Nomura Shōjirō (1879-1943), a Kyoto art dealer and textile merchant. He appreciated the uniqueness of traditional Japanese dress and devoted himself to the study and preservation of the most beautiful robes at a time when, because of the consumer demand for Western fashion, there was little interest in Japanese costume. His collection includes 156 complete robes and 120 screens on which are mounted fragments of robes in such a way as to suggest the whole garment; the first seventy-three robes and screens in the exhibition at the North Carolina Museum of Art are a part of this magnificent collection.

Kimono academies have been established in the past two decades which teach women the art of wearing the kimono, not simply how to put on a kimono but how to reflect the spirit that is an aspect of wearing the kimono: "in the manner and movements appropriate to the one who wears it and in the sensitivity to life and nature the kimono fosters." As long as tradition is such an integral part of the Japanese character, the kimono will have an artistic and sociological importance to the Japanese people.

Richard S. Schneiderman
Director, North Carolina Museum of Art

Acknowledgments

The exhibition "Robes of Elegance: Japanese Kimonos of the Sixteenth through Twentieth Centuries" and the catalogue which accompanies it have been made possible only through the support and talents of many individuals and organizations in Japan and the United States.

Through the support and stimulus of Department of Cultural Resources Secretary Patric Dorsey, this project has come to fruition. The National Museum of Japanese History, Sakura, and the National Museum of Modern Art, Tokyo, made the exhibition possible through their generous loans of some of Japan's most prized treasures, the *kosode* and kimonos that form the exhibition. Special thanks are extended to Tsuchida Naoshige, Director-General of the National Museum of Japanese History, and his staff, which includes Udagawa Takehisa, Professor of Japanese History; Tanaka Minoru, Director of the Museum Science Department; Akabane Noboru, Chief of the Division of Collections Management and Library Division; and Kikuchi Hiroo, Director of Administration. Thanks are also extended to Murayama Matsuo, Director-General of the Tokyo National Museum, and his staff, which includes Imanaga Seijirō, Chief Curator, Applied Arts Department; Nagasaki Iwao, Assistant Curator; Hasebe Gakuji, Director, Curatorial Board; Washizuka Hiromitsu, Chief Curator, Programming Department; and Nishikawa Kyōtarō, Deputy Director-General.

We are deeply grateful to the authors of this catalogue, Maruyama Nobuhiko, who is Research Associate in the Object Research Division of the Museum Science Department of the National Museum of Japanese History, and Ishimura Hayao, who is Chief Research Worker in the Applied Arts Department of the National Museum of Modern Art, for their expertise and scholarship, which have enabled us to enrich the exhibition with a catalogue. This gratitude is extended to Yamanobe Tomoyuki, former Curator of the Textiles Section, Tokyo National Museum, for his additions to the catalogue.

When this exhibition existed only as a fond wish, the earliest contacts with Japanese officials were made through Kakudo Yoshiko, Curator of Japanese Art, Asian Art Museum of San Francisco, with the valuable assistance of Rand Castile, Director. Negotiations for the exhibition first began in Japan with

Imanaga Seijirō, Chief Curator, Tokyo National Museum. Later discussions were held with the cooperation of the Agency for Cultural Affairs (Bunkachō), Yamamoto Nobuyoshi, Director, Fine Arts Division, and his staff, which includes Kawakami Skigeki, Usui Kuniaki, and Hiroi Yuichi.

The North Carolina Department of Commerce provided the Museum with vital assistance, especially its Tokyo office, Walter Johnson, Director. Mr. Johnson's assistant, Asakura Kumiko, served as translator during the first two negotiatory trips to Japan made by Secretary Dorsey and me. In the Raleigh office, Shirley Glover assisted in the transmission of documents between Raleigh and Japan. The guidance and hospitality of a good friend in Kyoto, Professor Glen Kaufman, was instrumental in the inclusion of contemporary kimonos in the exhibition. He, with Mrs. Sachiko Usui, Program Specialist, Kyoto American Center, scheduled visits to kimono artists' studios.

Many individuals shared advice and counsel that was essential for me to successfully traverse cultural and bureaucratic corridors: Dr. Sherman Lee, Chapel Hill; Professors John Sylvester and John Kelly, Japan Center, North Carolina State University, Raleigh; Alan Donaldson, North Carolina State University School of Textiles, Raleigh; Warren Obluck, Cultural Attaché, American Embassy, Tokyo; Dr. Eric J. Gangloff, Japan-United States Friendship Commission, Tokyo.

We are indebted to Margo Paul Ernst for her significant editorial assistance with the catalogue manuscript. Ms. Ernst was editor and contributor to *KOSODE: 16th-19th Century Textiles from the Nomura Collection*, which was published by the Japan Society and Kodansha International in conjunction with an exhibition shown at the Japan House Gallery, New York City, in 1984.

This exhibition would not be possible without the generous financial support of such foundations and businesses as American Airlines, the National Endowment for the Arts, a federal agency, and the North Carolina Museum of Art Foundation. We are grateful to DNP (America) for their assistance in publishing this catalogue.

Two individuals to whom we owe a tremendous debt of gratitude are Nishihata Shizuka Sakurai, who served not only as a translator but as our project coordinator in Japan, and Haruko Ward, who translated the catalogue and served as translator for the pre-exhibition visit to the Museum by Professor Udagawa.

My thanks also are extended to the staff of this institution, who put in many, many long days to bring this project to full blossom and whose talents ensure its success. It is my hope that the grandness of this exhibition repays the many who have contributed to it, and that it fulfills its original mission: to show our audiences the wealth and beauty of Japanese culture and to serve as a visible symbol of the friendship between the people of Japan and North Carolina.

Richard S. Schneiderman
Director, North Carolina Museum of Art

Maruyama Nobuhiko
Research Associate, Museum Science Department
National Museum of Japanese History

The Nomura Collection, which forms the base of the exhibition, is an extensive collection of garments and ornaments assembled by an art dealer from Kyoto, Nomura Shōjirō (1879–1943), before World War II. The collection of 595 items includes *kosode*, screens on which are mounted partial *kosode*, *obi*, combs, hair ornaments, bags, toilet articles, and other objects. The 156 *kosode* and 100 *kosode* screens that form the nucleus of the collection enjoy a great reputation as a resource which spans several hundred years, from the end of the Muromachi period to the early Meiji period.

The *kosode* screens, which are unique to this collection, are two-panel screens onto which fragile *kosode* fragments were pasted. The *kosode* were backed with paper and mounted as a collage in the *tagasode* (literally, "whose sleeves") style of the early premodern age. *Tagasode* is the name given to a type of screen popular in the seventeenth century in which the central elements were painted *kosode* draped casually on racks. These screens suggested the presence of an unseen beautiful woman. One hundred of Nomura's *kosode* collage screens are preserved in the National Museum of Japanese History in Sakura and one screen is preserved in the Tokusei Temple in Kyoto. Some fragments of the extant *kosode* not used for the collage on the screen also remain. Unfortunately, the texture of the material changed and the original designs were not always clear once the ancient *kosode* fragments had been pasted to the screens. Many of the *kosode* which Nomura reassembled were fragments which had been cut and sewn patchwork-style into Buddhist altar cloths and the like. He spent years collecting fragments of early pieces so that he could reproduce as much of the *kosode* as possible. Nomura's ingenuity in creating a new form of collage to prevent precious *kosode* fragments from being scattered and lost should be appreciated.

The items which Mr. Nomura collected were kept by his family after his death without the loss of a single fragment. The items left Japan around 1955, when the Nomura family emigrated to America, and the Nomura Collection gained popularity in the United States. In 1956 a portion of the collection was exhibited at The Metropolitan Museum of Art in New York, and in 1959 the entire collection was shown there. *Life* magazine reported that the exhibition was extremely popular and influenced fashion at the time.

The desire among Japanese people to have the Nomura Collection returned to Japan was heightened as word of the collection's popularity in America spread. In addition, new innovations and discoveries in the field of textiles during the 1960s aroused interest in traditional textiles. The Nomura family also wanted the return of the collection to Japan. Thanks to the efforts of interested parties, the Nomura Collection was acquired by the Bunkachō (Agency for Cultural Affairs) and returned to Japan after twenty years abroad.

The first exhibition of the Nomura Collection was held in 1941 at the Kyoto National Museum and was titled "*Jidai Kosode Hinagagata Byōbu*" ("Traditional *Kosode* Sample Screens"). In 1976, upon the return of the collection from America, many works from the collection, including the *kosode* screens, were displayed in the special exhibition "Japanese Textiles" at the Tokyo National Museum. The next exhibition of this collection was at the Japan House Gallery in New York City in the spring of 1984. It was titled "*Kosode* from the Nomura Shōjirō Collection."

The Nomura Collection was owned by the Tokyo National Museum until 1983, when ownership was transferred to the National Museum of Japanese History. Interest in the collection around the world has been strong, and the collection has occasionally been loaned to other countries.

Kosode of the Premodern Age

Maruyama Nobuhiko

Research Associate, Museum Science Department

National Museum of Japanese History

Introduction

Japan's cultural life developed under the influence of the continent of China in many significant respects, including religion, art, food, and architecture. Japanese clothing was no exception; its roots can be traced back to the Zui and Tō cultures of China. But at the end of the ninth century, official communication with Tō was broken off. Japan seized this opportunity to free itself, including its dress, from Chinese influence and began to walk a separate path. By the sixteenth century a distinctively Japanese style of dress, which included the wearing of *kosode* robes as outer garments, was born.

Kosode, a general term for kimonos worn until the end of the Edo period, are quite similar in cut to their modern counterparts. *Kosode* literally means "small or narrow sleeves," small in comparison to kimonos with wide sleeves made of two pieces of material sewn together (*ōsode*). The *ōsode* were outer garments routinely worn by the members of upper classes, which consisted of the aristocrats and warrior class, until the mid-fifteenth century. Originally, *kosode* were worn as undergarments by the upper classes. The common people, however, found *kosode* to be simpler and less restrictive than *osode* and wore them as outer garments. By the late sixteenth century, *kosode* were worn as outer garments without distinction to class.

Kosode is distinctive as clothing in its extraordinary decorativeness, which is beyond compare to anything in the Orient or even beyond. The design motif of a *kosode* is just as important, perhaps more important, than its function as a piece of clothing. In a word, *kosode* are canvases meant to be worn for their designs. This concept is more akin to the Western concept of "fine art" as opposed to "applied art."

The *kosode* is shaped from a single bolt of silk, which in modern times is about 36 centimeters wide. The garment is cut only across its width to form the finished layout, and the design elements, which are often applied while the silk is a single bolt, are not interrupted by cutting as with Western dress. As a result of straight line cutting, an open, flat *kosode* has sleeves and a body that unfold to form a single, continuous canvas. The two overlapping hems on each side of the garment also are extensions of this single pictorial frame. Western dress, in contrast, is cut with a curved line and a single pattern is copied on the cloth generally without consideration of its placement on the garment layout. The uninterrupted expanse of the *kosode* surface is well suited to the bold and complex designs of *kosode* decoration.

When we look through *kosode* fashion books (*hiinakata*) of the Edo period, we find that *kosode* design had its source in the refined and complex Japanese culture. In the images of the *kosode*, drawn from nature, the skill of nature itself is reflected. In the Edo period, beautiful *kosode* designs were important adjuncts to the popular woodblock prints (*ukiyoe*) and popular literature by such authors as Ihara Saikaku. The taste for *kosode* was deeply and widely rooted in the daily lives of the moneyed and ruling classes of Japanese society in the sixteenth through nineteenth centuries, and thus the cultural significance of *kosode* is considerable. That tradition is still inherent in the Japanese culture of today.

Conception and Technique in Premodern Kosode *Design*

In order for a *kosode* to be produced successfully, design ideas and production techniques must work in concert; this is essential to the creative process.

Sometimes ideas take the lead over technique, while at other times improvements in techniques precede and result in new design ideas. When both ideas and technique are combined, an exceptionally beautiful robe is created which transcends its function as clothing. The nature and quality of the relationship between design and technique has varied from era to era throughout Japanese history.

In studying the evolution of the relationship between ideas and the techniques in premodern *kosode*, a major development appears to have occurred during the Genroku years (1688–1704). Before the Genroku era *kosode* were designed through the use of previously existing techniques. After the Genroku period, newly invented techniques resulted in many design ideas that would have been impossible to realize just years before. It was with this fact in mind that this exhibition, "Robes of Elegance: Japanese Kimonos of the Sixteenth through Twentieth Centuries," was divided into two distinct periods.

The first period represented in the exhibition begins in the sixteenth century and extends through the early eighteenth century. During this period the basic decoration techniques were traditional ones: resist dyeing (*shibori*) and embroidery. Although popular, applied decoration was considered to be of poorer quality than woven decoration, which was fashionable before the seventeenth century, when *ōsode* were popular. Resist decoration was used mainly to dye the clothing of the common people and was considered inappropriate for official occasions. However, by the premodern period, in the sixteenth century, resist decoration rose to greater acceptance and was regarded as the basic *kosode* decorating technique in the form of *tsujigahana*, a developed form of *shibori*, and *nuihaku*, a technique combining embroidery and applied metallic leaf (*surihaku*).

With this technical development, new effects, unattainable with previously existing weaving techniques, were achieved. The advances in development were not without their limits, however, especially in the expression of concrete objects or precise details of motifs. For example, in premodern times, it was almost impossible to illustrate acute-angled motifs or clear outlines with resist dyeing. Expressing curved lines and subtle shades through embroidery was exceptionally difficult as well. Even so, up until the early

5

part of the eighteenth century, the makers of *kosode* skillfully used the available techniques to success-fully create the complicated designs that seem impossible to duplicate even today. It can be said that the techniques of resist dyeing and embroidery were refined to their purest forms during the sixteenth and seventeenth centuries, when every possible aspect of these techniques was explored.

Although the production of *kosode* during the sixteenth century was fraught with technical limitations, the late seventeenth century was a time when techniques spurred conception. By the end of the seven-teenth century the stagnant culture of the military elite and warrior class was replaced by the blossoming culture of the wealthy townsmen. Townsmen became the principle patrons of the business community, enjoying the decorative *kosode* and contributing ideas for new designs. Factors instrumental in bringing about this cultural shift were the rapid spread of *yūzen* (painted resist) dyeing and the popularity of the *kosode* fashion books of the Edo period. *Yūzen* dyeing made possible free expression similar to that of picture painting, including the rendering of minute details and complicated coloring. The technical limi-tations that had plagued artistic expression during the early period were erased by the effects *yūzen* dyeing afforded. In addition, *kosode* fashion books, which were being published in rapid succession, provided a constant supply of new ideas for the designer. They also served to stimulate more and more buyers to purchase decorative *kosode* of the latest style.

The peak period that resulted from *yūzen* dyeing and the advent of fashion books was short-lived. By the latter half of the eighteenth century, the intense experimentation with *yūzen* dyeing, coupled with the public saturation of the *kosode* fashion books, invited the exhaustion of ideas.

When comparing *kosode* of the sixteenth century to those of the late seventeenth century, a significant difference in the transformation of designs is evident. This is because the works belonging to the earlier period stand on successively transforming styles. In other words, *kosode* design until the beginning of the eighteenth century was a succession of period-specific styles, evident in the basic Momoyama period style, Keichō style, Kanbun style, and Genroku style. For instance, during the first half of the premodern period, only the military elite, warrior class, aristocrats, and very wealthy, privileged merchants wore decorative *kosode* in everyday life, and *kosode* design was dictated by their similar taste. The *yūzen*-dyed works that were an integral part of the later period contained such a variety of motifs and applied design techniques that classifying the works by design composition is impossible. Also, the rise of a new class of townsmen added diversity of taste to *kosode* decoration. However, from the latter half of the eighteenth century *kosode* decoration declined toward cliché as the shogunate and economy waned. With this transformation of styles in mind, I would like to review the works in the exhibition historically.

Tsujigahana *Design*

Along with *yūzen* dyeing, *tsujigahana*, which embraces a number of decorative techniques, is one of the most familiar terms for Japanese dyed materials. But while *yūzen* dyeing still is popular in contemporary Japan, *tsujigahana* dyeing, as it originally was done, has ceased—even the term's origin is not precisely known. For this reason it is sometimes called "dyed goods of illusion." Much of the ambiguity about *tsujigahana* dyeing results from the fact that contemporary *tsujigahana* dyeing does not correspond to the *tsujigahana* dyeing of premodern times.

Originally, *tsujigahana* dyeing was used to express concrete motifs through *shibori* resist dyeing, applied gold leaf (*surihaku*), brush painting (*kakie*), and embroidery. The material used was silk, especially *nerinuki*, a simple-weave silk in which scoured raw silk threads were used for the weft and soft white silk threads (*renshi*) for the warp. Frequently used for *kosode* during the Momoyama period, *nerinuki* was thin, with a desirable tension and sheen. The term *tsujigahana*, as found in fourteenth- and fifteenth-century documents, was described as decorated summer *kosode*, with rouge dye, worn mainly by women and children. These unlined summer *kosode* generally were made of hemp or ramie. No connection between *tsujigahana* and *shibori* dyeing is made in these documents.

From the beginning of the premodern period, the elegant term *tsujigahana*, literally "roadside flowers," came to signify a dyed material totally different from the original *tsujigahana*. It is unclear when or why this type of dyed good came to be called *tsujigahana*. However, this type of dyed material, with *shibori* resist as its basis, was popular from the end of the Muromachi period to the early Edo period, and various excellent designs were produced for it. The *shibori* technique, which appears in what is called *tsujigahana* today, was as bold as it was sensitive. Through the use of thick, bleached hemp threads, the effects of the resist dye were strengthened as the outlines of complicated motifs were sewn and compressed. To reserve them in white, the motifs were twisted with bamboo skins, a technique known as capped (*bōshi*) *shibori*, and the unprotected areas were dyed. To gather the material for the resist, thick threads were sewn along the outlines of the area to be reserved from the dye. The thin silk was sometimes damaged by the threads used for the resist, and in some rare cases, these threads remain, for to remove them would have damaged the material. The sewing for the resist had to be extremely secure to assure that the dye would not penetrate its boundaries. *Shibori* resist techniques were used with great liberty because they allowed the artisan more freedom of design than was previously possible.

Tsujigahana design as I have described it above can be categorized into three groups, as follows, according to the amount of *shibori* in the entire decoration and the techniques used to achieve it:

1. Designs of comparatively simple composition and naïve taste, with conspicuously blurred dye caused by loosely controlled *shibori* resist dyeing.

2. Designs with motifs of complicated design carefully articulated by precise *shibori* resist dyeing, with large amounts of brush painting (*kakie*), applied gold leaf (*surihaku*), and embroidery, creating a colorful impression.

3. Designs which, through the use of high-quality *shibori* techniques, freely express

clear motifs without supplementary methods, such as brush painting (*kakie*), and
which show a refined sense of design, even though the design may be one-dimensional.

These three groups are classified by the characteristics of the designs, not by chronological order. For example, the blurred dye, which is one of the characteristics of the first category, could be the result of primitive technique, or it can be regarded as signifying a culture's ebb. That kind of naïveté, however, is one of the charms of *tsujigahana* design, and it is thought that in some cases the effect of the blurred dye was consciously dramatized. From the viewpoint that the technique advanced as time went by, one would expect to find *tsujigahana* design of the latest period in the third category. Actually, no clue exists among the remaining works to indicate when the peak period of *tsujigahana* took place. Because the chronology of developments in *tsujigahana* cannot be delineated with certainty, the presentation of *tsujigahana* design must be limited to just these three groups here.

Nuihaku

Another method of dyeing that was used beautifully alongside *tsujigahana* during the premodern age is *nuihaku*. *Nuihaku* is a technique which combines embroidery in many colors with gold or silver leaf, thereby achieving luxurious effects. The term also refers to *kosode* decorated by this technique. The main component of *nuihaku* is embroidery, which, although arduous, allows great freedom in pictorial decoration. *Shūbutsu* (embroidered Buddhas), which were produced frequently during the Nara period, are good examples of the pictorial effects possible with embroidery. However, among the *nuihaku* of the Momoyama period, the motifs in many works show an intentional artistic restraint. These embroidered works resemble weavings with regular and repeated motifs. The float-stitch embroidery technique called *watashi*, with its long and puffy bridges, was used to attain the lustrous, three-dimensional effect of brocade. *Watashi* is thought to be another type of embroidery prevalent mostly during the Momoyama period.

From the evidence that exists it appears that *nuihaku* originated as a substitute for high-quality woven designs containing complex compositions produced through complicated techniques. The production of these weavings became difficult after a significant battle during the late fifteenth century.

The origin of *nuihaku* differs from that of *tsujigahana* design, which had its beginnings in the simple *shibori* dyeing of the common people. Weaving production declined during the wars of the sixteenth century, but after peace was restored in the seventeenth century, *nuihaku* ceased to be an imitation of weaving and began to include design expressions specific to embroidery.

During premodern times, *nuihaku* of the Momoyama period (1573–1615) and *nuihaku* of the Edo period (1615–1868) reflected different tastes. The traditional basic style of decoration from the fifteenth century was retained in *nuihaku* of the Momoyama period. This basic style also was found in the following designs: *kata-suso*, in which the design was placed on the shoulder and skirt areas, separated from other areas by straight lines or lines resembling the seashore, leaving the areas around the waist blank; *dangawari*, in which the surface of the *kosode* was divided into several bands (*dan*) by horizontal lines to the center seam in the back (*senui*), with different patterns placed in each band; and *sō-moyō* (allover), with motifs covering the entire *kosode* surface. The success of these designs depended on geometric regularities, such as bilateral symmetry and repetition, original forms of which can be seen in drawings of clothing contained in the picture scrolls (*emaki*) of the Kamakura period.

Nuihaku in the Momoyama period had reached its peak and could be easily differentiated from the woven designs that it emulated. Motifs that could not be expressed in weaving, such as small birds swimming among the water grass, or a field full of autumn wildflowers, now could be depicted with great realism by *nuihaku*. When one looks at the whole *kosode* from a distance, one notices that the vividly embroidered details are perfectly assimilated into the whole composition. The balanced effect of woven patterns was the inspiration behind the early *nuihaku kosode*, on whose surfaces patterns were applied.

During the Edo period asymmetry was favored over symmetry for its greater movement and variety in composition. As the popularity of evenly positioned motifs declined, *nuihaku* was used to create designs distinct from those akin to woven decoration. In addition, the amount of applied gold leaf (*surihaku*) increased and was used in detailed patterning instead of just the filling of the ground between each motif. *Rinzu* silk, which is actually figured satin, became the preferred material in this period, replacing the *nerinuki* plain-weave silk of the Momoyama period. Another notable new characteristic of Edo period *nuihaku kosode* was the frequent use of *shibori*.

The big changes that took place in *nuihaku* decoration between the Momoyama and Edo periods were caused indirectly by societal upheaval, which prompted changes in the standards of beauty. During the latter half of the Momoyama period, called the Keichō years (1596–1615), a consecutive series of events that would determine the future of premodern Japan took place: the death of the great warlord and father of the Imperial adviser, Toyotomi Hideyoshi; the battle of Sekigahara; and the winter and summer battles at Osaka. These events marked a major turning point in the cultural history of Japan, along with its political and economic structure. Reflecting these changes in society, clothing styles changed greatly after the Keichō years. The following passage from *Keichō Kenbunki*, an anthology of essays written in 1614, provides an observation of trends in public costume:

> Not only the great warlords of today but warriors of every class are concerned with beauty, wearing ryorakinshu (colorfully woven and embroidered fine silks).

> The warriors also decorate themselves according to their status, carefully making up their appearance, and spending all their pay on clothing. It is a peaceful time now, so they put their arrows away in quivers, and swords in boxes and devote themselves solely to worldly pleasures. It is just amazing to hear of and see these beautiful robes everywhere. Such things were unheard of before.

This account tells us that even the lower-class warriors competed for luxurious materials and colorful designs and enjoyed beautiful clothing. It is known that after the war at Sekigahara, as the preoccupation with fighting and battle dissipated, people's attention rapidly returned to daily life. Their strong interest in their daily customs guided design away from tradition and forward to a new style peculiar to the Edo period.

The Keichō Style

It was the Keichō (1596–1615) style of *nuihaku*, rising above the traditional construction and regularity of previous years, that heralded the arrival of the Edo period (1615–1867) in *kosode* design. There were similar elements of this style of *nuihaku* in the early part of the Edo period as well: the use of *rinzu* (figured satin), assymetrical composition of different varieties, and the addition of decoration in mostly dark colors. The Keichō style was different in that the intricate beauty of *kosode* was dramatized by an intertwining of every technique in decoration. The whole surface of Keichō style *kosode* was divided (*somewake*) into several areas dyed in crimson, black, or, as was often the case, *kurobeni* (reddish dark brown). Characteristic of this style were complicated abstract forms in which various motifs of trees, flowers, birds, musical instruments, and scenery were embroidered or dyed by *shibori*. Generally, the sequential or perspective relationships between the motifs, as well as their literal context, were totally ignored. Consequently, what these motifs were meant to represent often cannot be understood clearly today. The empty spaces on the ground between the motifs were filled with detailed patterns, such as the tortoise-shell and gold-leaf haze patterns. *Kosode* in which densely positioned motifs covered the whole surface, hiding the ground, are called *jinashi* (without background) *kosode*. Keichō style *kosode* were the most luxurious of *jinashi kosode*.

The frequent use of *shibori* in the Keichō style reminds one of its relationship to *tsujigahana* design. The fragment of *kosode* with fan papers and wild flowers (No. 4, right) is an example of the Keichō style, but the motifs of the fan and the cloud shapes made through *shibori* dyeing rather resemble the motifs in the *kosode* remnant with scattered fans made through *tsujigahana* dyeing (No. 2). However, where Keichō style *shibori* reflects a concentration in *somewake* (dyeing in divided areas) over the entire surface of the *kosode*, *tsujigahana* design was devoted to concrete objective expression. The positioning of the motifs in *tsujigahana* design was limited to a few basic forms, such as scattered motifs (*chirashi moyō*) or motifs on shoulders and skirt (*kata-suso*). In *tsujigahana* mainly bright colors were applied, with *nerinuki* (plain-weave) silk as the principal ground material. The contrast between *kosode* of the Momoyama and Keichō periods can be recognized thus in *tsujigahana*.

One should not consider the Keichō style to have been limited to the years of the Keichō era (1596–1615), although that name is used to describe the style. The peak of the Keichō style appears to have occurred during the Kanei era (1624–43), when the culture of the Edo period was being established. The difference between *kosode* design of the Edo period represented in the Keichō style and that of the Momoyama style was stated earlier, and the same differentiating elements can be seen in their shape. In general, the *kosode* of the Momoyama period had relatively narrow sleeve width compared to the body width, and had short *yuki* (the length from the center of the back to the sleeve opening). The ratios of the measurements of each part of the *kosode* changed drastically during the seventeenth century. The ratios established after the eighteenth century are comparable to the measurements of today's kimono. Keichō style *kosode* had a narrow body width and a contrastingly long sleeve width and *yuki*, nearly resembling the *kosode* of the post-eighteenth century.

Kosode design after the early premodern age changed in response to the interaction of various decorative techniques and styles: *nuihaku* of the Momoyama period versus *tsujigahana* design, *kosode* of the Momoyama period versus *kosode* of the Keichō style, *nuihaku* of the upper class versus *kosode* of the common people and townsmen. The change of *kosode* during this period of approximately 100 years can be understood in the context of social changes in Japan at that time: the waning of the feudal culture, the decline of the warrior class and its culture, and the rising of townsmen to power. In that sense the abstractness of the Keichō style may be considered a reflection of the confusion of the contemporary social situation. While it is true that, historically, the Keichō style stood in between the basic style of the Momoyama period and the later Kanbun style (which will be described later), the Keichō style was not just an "in-between" phenomenon whose unique qualities are undeserving of attention. The Keichō style was both the final goal of the spirit of a time that sought the flamboyant decoration described in *Keichō Kenbunki* and a witness to the ultimate potential of dyeing techniques.

The Kanbun Style

The transition from a time of great social upheaval to the social stability of the mid-seventeenth century was symbolically reflected in *kosode* design. The overcrowded *jinashi nuihaku* ("without background" *kosode* with applied metallic leaf and embroidery) peculiar to the Keichō style were alternated by *kosode* with much more simplified designs of the Kanbun style. Reduced colors, large scale motifs placed in contrasting positions in a boldly composed space, and asymmetry became characteristics of the simpler Kanbun *kosode*. Along with the Keichō period, the Kanbun period (1661–73) is considered a landmark era in the cultural history of the early half of the Edo period. Although two *kosode* styles bear the names of historical periods, the so-called Keichō style was not limited to the Keichō years alone; it is recognized as a characteristic style of the early Edo period in general. On the other hand, the Kanbun style represents only the works created during the Kanbun years. The use of the term *Kanbun* to describe this particular style of *kosode* follows from the fact that all the extant examples of *kosode* designs during the Kanbun years present the characteristics of a particular style. There are two very important anthologies of *kosode* designs which contain examples of the Kanbun style. They are the *Karigane-ya* anthologies of garment designs, dated 1661 and 1663–64, and a fashion book called *On Hiinakata*, published in 1666. *Karigane-ya* is a record of the personal sketches drawn by a dry goods dealer named Karigane-ya, who received orders and prepared designs for the garments for Tōfukumon-in, daughter of the second shogun Tokugawa Hidetada and second queen of the Emperor Go-suio, and her household. These drawings are preserved in the City Museum of Osaka and the Kawashima Weaving Research Institute in Kyoto. Most of the 600 designs reflect the characteristics of the Kanbun style. These underdrawings are a very important source because of their attached notes, which listed the names of the kimono wearers, the dates of the orders and their completion, as well as instructions pertaining to the quality and color of the materials and technical processes. From the information given in these notes it is known that *kosode* were created faithfully according to the sketches and that the designs in the Kanbun style were cherished by the highest strata of society at that time. Karigane-ya was both a first-class dry goods dealer and the head of a family of great artists. He was related to the famous painter Hon-ami Kōetsu and father to the brothers Ogata Kōrin and Ogata Kenzan, who admired Kōetsu and became the representative masters of the decorative arts in Japan. It is supposed that Karigane-ya had a major role in composing new designs.

On Hiinakata was edited by Shoritsuzan Taichibei of Kyoto in August 1666. Of the 200 *kosode* designs included therein, the Kanbun style is recognizable in about 170. No proof exists, as it does with the privately created *Karigane-ya* anthology, that the designs in the published *On Hiinakata* were ever made, faithfully or otherwise, into *kosode*. However, to suppose that these designs constituted the actual fashion of the day is probably correct, for some instructional notes regarding the technical aspects of the *kosode*-making processes, although not detailed, were included. In addition, the fashion books which were influenced by *On Hiinikata* were published one after another. The designs in *On Hiinakata* distinctively expressed new motifs concisely and plainly and apparently reflected accurately the taste of the townsmen. Both the privately prepared design anthologies and the published fashion books delineated the style on which these distinctive Kanbun designs were based, and at the same time encouraged a thriving fashion industry.

Both embroidery and *shibori* dyeing, prevalent during the previous period, were the basic techniques used in creating the Kanbun style. However, where the preceding Keichō period saw the frequent use of *jinashi nuihaku*, a style in which the motifs were so densely packed that the ground virtually became invisible, the Kanbun style included motifs that were larger in size, and the spaces between the motifs were left undecorated. Why such contrasting styles appeared in succession may appear at first baffling, until one recognizes the great influence that the "*Furisode* Fire," the mammoth fire of 1657, had on Japanese society. The fire destroyed many dry goods stores and dye-weave studios, preventing the production of elaborate designs, and it was inevitable that the motifs would be simplified. The resultant reduction in labor helps explain the sudden appearance of a new syle, the Kanbun style. There are many examples of *kosode* which stand in a transitional position between the Keichō and Kanbun styles, presenting the characteristics of both styles. In general it is difficult for a designer to leave a space undecorated. Many designers, especially Western designers, tend to "fill the empty spaces" in a decorated surface. Exceptional artistic ability and experience are necessary for a designer to utilize an empty space effectively. It can be said that the Keichō style was born from the "fear of the empty space." It was a necessary rite of passage for the Keichō style to escape from the past curse of excessive decoration and to go through the transitional stage.

These examples suggest that there did exist a transition from the Keichō style to the Kanbun style. The transition was an unprecedentedly quick one. In only twenty to thirty years during the mid-seventeenth century, *kosode* design changed drastically. *Jinashi* (without ground) *nuihaku* (*kosode* with metallic leaf and embroidery) did not disappear overnight; however, by the latter half of the seventeenth century, *jinashi nuihaku* were considered out of date and only a limited number of people wore them. In *Shō En Tai-kan* (*Encyclopedia of Various Beauties*), which was published in 1684, it says:

A woman of forty-three or forty-four, wearing an ancient *jinashi* kimono and gold-leafed *obi*. . . . This is a daughter of the warrior who lives in the mansion at Tennachu.

In this transition from the Keichō to Kanbun style another notable change occurred in the nature of the *kosode* buyer. During this period townsmen became more prosperous and powerful. *Kosode* fashion trends were set no longer by the military elite but by the newly prosperous townsmen. Unfortunately there are no extant examples of *kosode* that were actually worn by the townsmen of the early Edo period, and so no comparative study is possible at present. In the genre paintings (*kan-ei fūzokuga*) that exist from that period, *kosode* very similar to Kanbun style *kosode* and the townsmen wearing them are vividly depicted. Such free designs originated by the townsmen stimulated the taste of the military elite, whose culture was waning. It is my theory that the military elite adapted the townsmen's designs for their own use, and this style later came to be known as the Kanbun style. The townspeople set into motion their overflowing creativity, transforming the quality of the fashion of the Edo period. Their creative energy developed into the Genroku style, a discussion of which follows.

The Genroku Style

During the peak of the Kanbun style, luxurious *shibori* dyed and embroidered *kosode* became subject to the sweeping sumptuary laws issued in 1683. Under the new laws, even the kinds of techniques applied to *kosode* production were strictly regulated. The use of gold threads, flashy colored embroidery, and allover *hitta shibori* was forbidden. But the laws could not prevent people from pursuing luxurious goods, and the effects of the laws were temporary. During the Genroku period (1688–1704) the wealthy townsmen's class finally won a position of cultural leadership, which traditionally had been held by the military elite, and with the establishment of the townsmen's culture came a new fashion.

In reviewing the transitions which took place between the basic and Keichō styles as well as between the Keichō and Kanbun styles, I have described the major shifts in taste which prompted new developments in design. Contrastingly, the transition from the Kanbun style to the Genroku style entailed no recognizable change in taste. Rather, the Genroku style is a developed form of the Kanbun style, and both basically possess the same elements. When compared to others, the Genroku style is a minor style not terribly distinct from the Kanbun style. A line must be drawn, however, between the Kanbun style and Genroku style, considering that some distinctive features belong only to the latter. I shall treat the Genroku style as an established style in its own right and elaborate on the two major differences which exist between the Genroku style and the Kanbun style.

The first distinguishing characteristic of the Genroku style is the undecorated ground remaining only around the left waist area on the back of the *kosode*. With the Kanbun as its basis, the composition of the Genroku style almost seems to reflect the cultural changes taking place: just as the townsmen's class advanced socially, *kosode* decorations advanced into empty spaces, leaving only a small amount of space undecorated, as described above. In contrast to the assymetrical balance of the Kanbun style, in which the central design was placed on either side of the upper body, the focal point of the Genroku style design moved to the lower body, adding stability. It should also be noted that the design of the front of the *kosode* became fuller, although in the Kanbun style the frontal design was not very significant. A symmetrical design was placed on the lower skirt of the front, extending to the back skirt, with the side seam as its axis. In the exhibition are typical examples of the Genroku style (Nos. 14, 15, 16, and 18). No. 35, which is an example of *yūzen* dyeing, also shows the composition of the Genroku style. As was stated above, the design of the Genroku style *kosode* includes a fuller skirt area and a balance in the lower body of the garment; however, when compared to the works created after the mid-eighteenth century, in which designs around the lower skirt (*susomoyō*) were drawn continuously from the left to the right overlap (*okumi*), the designs of the Genroku style skirt lacked the continuation of the motifs at the side seam line.

The second major characteristic of the Genroku style is a regimentation of design. As the amount of empty space decreased to accommodate the encroaching motifs, flexibility of composition became limited, resulting in *kosode* of similar composition. The plums in No. 14, cherries in No. 15, chrysanthemums in No. 21, and larches and wild oranges in Nos. 18 and 23 reflect how even motifs became notably standardized. Not surprisingly, every *kosode* in the Genroku style gives the impression of being similar to another, despite the differences in color. The Kanbun style, however, was distinctly dynamic, carefree, and wonderfully original. The eventual regimentation was caused not only by a reduction of labor in the face of ever-increasing demand, but also by the successively published *kosode hiinakata* (fashion books), which became increasingly available during the Genroku period. More and more publishers began to produce these fashion catalogues, which remarkably hastened the circulation of the new fashion and expanded its market; at the same time, however, it stifled creativity.

The Genroku style symbolizes the prosperity of the townsmen's culture. The circumstances surrounding the development of the style foreshadowed today's fashion industry. In that sense, it also would be inappropriate to classify the Genroku style as one variation of the Kanbun style. The Genroku style, with its embroidery and *shibori* dyeing, should be regarded as a fully matured stage of *kosode* design, distinct from the Kanbun style that sprang from an abundance of creative energy. The consecutive transformation of style since the beginning of the premodern age finally matured and came to completion in the Genroku style.

Kosode *at the End of the Premodern Age*

Yamanobe Tomoyuki
Former Curator, Textiles Section
Tokyo National Museum

The extreme flamboyancy and colorfulness of *yūzen* dyeing became overripe and decadent by the beginning of the nineteenth century. The improved and refined techniques caused the designs to become standardized and their content poor. In protest of the frequent sumptuary regulations imposed by the shogunal government, a new fashion was innovated among the townsmen. *Kosode* made by such techniques as striping (*shima*), ikat (*kasuri*), *chūgata* dyeing, and *komon* dyeing in darker colors of indigo blue, brown, and gray became fashionable, reflecting the chic and subdued taste of the townsmen.

During this period *kosode* worn by the women of the military elite class were called *goten-fū* (in palatial style). This style seems to have developed from the *chayatsuji* style, in which all the designs of summer *katabira* (unlined summer *kosode* of hemp) were dyed in indigo blue with reserved areas and embroidered. The designs in the palatial style were also called *gosyo-toki* (guessing game of the court), and were graceful but clichéd. Various literary works, such as poems, classic literature, and Nō theatre, were represented with allusive motifs. Women of the dignified military elite class demonstrated their education and social status by guessing rightly the allusions of the motifs of *kosode* worn by other women and by wearing *kosode* with such motifs themselves.

Another new *yūzen* technique which appeared at the end of the Edo period emulated paintings of the period. Actually, the designs were taken from the realistic paintings of the Shijō school, which were popular at the time. Compared with the colorfulness of other *yūzen* techniques, these were more subdued and graceful. This return to more classical themes was a reaction to the decadence of earlier styles of *kosode* decoration.

When the Meiji Restoration began (1868), drastic political changes took place in the new government. In this period, the national isolationist policy was abolished, and the country was opened to foreign influence. A drastic change occurred in Japanese clothing as Western culture poured into Japan. Western garments (*yōfuku*), completely alien to anything previously seen in Japan, were aggressively imported. As Japanese and Western style garments learned to co-exist, the term *kimono* (literally "thing worn") came to mean only Japanese style garments (*wafuku*). The term *kosode*, which had been used to signify Japanese style garments, became obsolete. Men's clothing immediately became *yōfuku* (Western style); women, however, continued to wear kimonos until the mid-twentieth century.

Some of the elements of the traditional kimono of the Edo period were retained in the kimono of the Meiji period. Because of the fall of the warrior class, kimonos in the palatial style faded away. Japanese style painters, who lost their jobs when the Western painting style was introduced and enthusiastically received, made their living by painting the underdrawings of the kimonos. Kimonos with classic designs by Japanese painters were popular until the end of the nineteenth century. The artists of the young generation who studied at art schools started a movement of "new style kimonos." They were influenced by the Art Nouveau movement in Europe. Decorations with motifs in curved lines, like trailing plants, swirls, and flowing water, became very popular. It is interesting to note that they included the re-imported designs of paintings with classic themes of flowers and birds (*kachōzu*) by Ogata Kōrin and Katsushika Hokusai, which provided the impetus for the Art Nouveau movement.

Finally I would like to briefly mention the kimono of the earlier half of the twentieth century, after the Taishō period. During the latter half of the nineteenth century the notion of large-scale capitalistic-based production was introduced. Large companies, department stores, and wholesale dealers started dealing with kimono producers. These organizations hired professional designers who produced in rapid succession kimonos with new designs. The designs were pluralistic in order to respond to the various tastes of the consumer. Some were traditonal in style, some were Chinese, others were Indian style, still others were European.

Yūzen *Dyeing*

Maruyama Nobuhiko
Research Associate, Museum Science Department
National Museum of Japanese History

What we call *yūzen* today signifies a dyeing technique in which various designs are resisted by fine lines of paste and dyed in various colors. The term also applies to dyed products created via this technique.

The steps involved in *yūzen* dyeing can be summarized as follows. Resist paste, which is made primarily from glutinous rice, is squeezed out of a funnel-shaped tube with a mouthpiece and applied to the outlines of the designs, a process called tube painting (*tsutsugaki*). Then dyes are applied within the outlines, a step referred to as "blushing" (*irosashi*). The process of resisting the designs by paste, called *noribuse*, follows. Next, the ground is dyed by brush painting. The material is steamed, washed in water, and processed further to be finished. Other *yūzen* dyeing techniques exist, such as "toothpick" paste (*yōjinori*), in which very glutinous paste is applied by thin twigs instead of tubes, as well as stencil *yūzen* and copying *yūzen*, which have been developed since the Meiji period.

During the latter half of the seventeenth century, however, *yūzen* did not signify dyed products, but must have been associated with fan painting by Miyazaki Yūzen. Miyazaki Yūzen is said to have lived in Chion-in-mae in Kyoto and died in 1711. Although it was after him that *yūzen* dyeing was named, he was originally a fan painter. His fan paintings are known to have been popular among city people from the Tenna-Teikyo period to the Genroku period from the fact that they are talked about as brand name products in such novels as *Kōshoku Ichidai Otoko* (*The Man Who Spent His Life at Lovemaking*), written by Ihara Saikaku in 1682; *Kōshoku-Sandai Otoko* (*The Man Who Enjoyed Three Generations of Lovemaking*), written by the same author in 1686; *Jinrin Kunmō Zui* (*The Anthology of Pictures of Moral Teachings*), written in 1690; and *Jinrin Juhoki* (*The Very Important Moral Teachings*), written in 1696.

Encouraged by the popularity of his fan paintings, Yūzen started to design *kosode* around the Teikyō period. The first document which associates Yūzen's name with *kosode* designs is the preface of *Shokoku Onhiinakata* (*Fashions of Each State*), published in 1686, which reads: ". . . recently popular in the capital city is the *yūzen* style . . . ." The book's table of contents lists a section titled "*Yūzen* Style." In *Genji Hiinakata* (*Genji Fashion Book*), which was published the following year, 1687, various dyeing techniques were introduced. Among the statements there is a line which reads: "*yūzen* dyeing is in fashion not only on fans but on *kosode*, which can be seen with a design of evening glories in dry goods shops along the Gojō street . . . ." This tells us that *yūzen* dyeing for *kosode* was developed from its application to fan painting.

A more detailed account of this development is found in the preface of *Onna-yō Kunmō Zui* (*Moral Teachings for Women*), which was published in 1687:

> There was a painter who was called Yūzen. He painted first-class paintings on the fans, which delighted men and women of all classes. By this he came to understand the people's taste. He created designs for the women's *kosode* and offered them to a certain dry goods dealer. Because he heard that these interested the people, a certain book dealer published these widely.

This tells us the story of how, again, the application of the popular fan paintings to *kosode* designs by fan painter Yūzen was received enthusiastically. The phrase "a certain book dealer published these widely" indicates that the designs perhaps were published in a *kosode* fashion book.

Among the *kosode* fashion books published prior to that year only the above-mentioned *Shokoku Onhiinakata* records the term *yūzen*. In 1688 a person named Yūjinsai Kiyochika, who seems to have been one of the disciples of Yūzen, published *Yūzen Hiinakata* (*Yūzen Fashion Book*). In the preface to this book it says:

> There is a person named Miyazaki Yūzen whose skills in drawing are excellent beyond description. He is not only able to create refined traditional designs but also knows how to appeal to the modern beautiful taste. From the most upper-class madames, who are kept in the closet, so to speak, to the lower-class women, with bare feet, and even young girls, his designs are sought after as the most fashionable.

It is known from this record that, by the Teikyō years, *yūzen* designs had been enthusiastically praised by women regardless of their class.

Thus *yūzen* became the new mode of *kosode* designs. *Yūzen* of this time, however, refers not to the *yūzen* dyeing technique now familiar to us but to the designs which the painter Yūzen created. What characteristics did these designs share? The above-mentioned *Shokoku Onhiinakata* lists two examples of "*yūzen* designs" in a chapter on styles of designs of Kyoto townsmen. In the entries the designs are explained as "*yūzen* designs of a blossom in a circle" and "blossoms of four seasons in a circle." From this it is known that a major characteristic of the *yūzen* design was its circular forms. In addition, *Onna Juhoki* (*Important Things for Women*), published in 1693, described *yūzen* designs as circular in a chapter titled "About Clothing, Especially Dyed Goods":

> The city fashion of the capital city naturally changes as the time goes by. All the big hits which appear from time to time are gone in five to eight years. Such fashions as *koshikizome* by Yoshinaga of Nakahi, *yūzen* dyeing circles, *yamamichisuzaki* by Hachimonjiya of Kamikyō, *uchidashi-kanoko* of Shimokyō dyeing seem already old-fashioned and unrefined by now.

The author of *Yūzen Hiinakata*, Yujinsai, boasts in his preface that he had mastered the *yūzen* style. This book records quite a few circular designs, although these are not just simple circles. Many circles are arranged with concrete motifs of tortoise shells (*kikko*), pine bark lozenges (*shobishi*), cedar doors, fan papers, round fans, butterflies, and shells. It was a natural outcome that Yūzen and his school of *yūzen* designers excelled in their overall *kosode* design, in which small motifs were united to make middle-sized motifs, because they were experts in the decoration of small spaces such as fans.

On the other hand fashion books related to *yūzen* designs, such as *Yojō Hinakata* (*Charming*), published by Yūzen himself in 1692, and the above-mentioned *Yūzen Hiinakata*, include quite a few pictorial designs, such as mountain scenes and carp confronting a waterfall. While the materials themselves are not new, the fluent and flexible technique evident in brush painting is clearly distinguished from the designs of other fashion books. Kitamura Shinsetsu, quoting from "*Wanku Monogatari*" ("Story of Wanku") in his *Kiyūshōran* (*Funny Stories*), says:

> Genji, in his long white satin coat decorated by ink painting of *yūzen* of Kyoto was very conspicuous. It was alright to be that way then, because they had not yet had sumptuary laws against clothing.

Kitamura concludes, "Drawing on clothing has been traditional, but this one became popular because it was done in ink painting. A certain Yūzen originated this." It is doubtful that Yūzen originated this, but it is admitted that Yūzen was excellent in painting *kosode*.

From the facts mentioned above, the major characteristics of *kosode* designs in the *yūzen* style can be considered to have been circular designs developed from fan paintings and fluent pictorial designs. How does the kind of *yūzen* design described above relate to what we call the *yūzen* dyeing technique, with its fine lines of paste? An answer can be found in *Yūzen Hiinakata*, which lists the characteristics of *yūzen* dyeing as follows:

> 1. In *yūzen* dyeing favorite motifs are first sketched. Paste is applied, then the ground

is tie-dyed in various colors. The blurs of the tie-dyed outlines are not corrected. Painting is added.

2. The dyes do not dissolve in water. They can be used on any silk materials.

3. The regular dyes would not paint clearly and blurred on the red silk. Now painting is possible.

4. Colored paints and applied gold and silver leaf are used in painting *kosode*, summer kimonos (*katabira*), *obi* belts and other kinds of belts, and wrappers. Bathrobes (*yokui*), *furoshiki* wrappers, and long handkerchiefs (*sanjaku-tenugui*) are dyed in *somewake* (divided background), and the motifs are reserved in white.

5. Besides clothing, almost everything, including incense wrappers, perfume bags, *shikishi*-frame papers, *tanzaku* papers, pocket papers, pocket fans, wooden boxes, fire pails, papier-mâché boxes, stationery boxes, combs, and wine cups, has some type of cute decoration.

The most interesting and revealing item is the first one, which states: "In *yūzen* dyeing favorite motifs are first sketched. Paste is applied . . . ." Here, for the first time, *yūzen* dyeing and the application of paste are related. In *Yūzen Hiinakata* technical instructions are written in the upper margin of each design. Among the 121 *kosode* designs described, thirty-three of them contain instructions for "paste application." From this it is confirmed that paste resist was characteristic to *yūzen*. The technique of resist by paste application has a long history, and was not originated by Yūzen. Examples with paste resist remain from as early as the fourteenth and fifteenth centuries.

Special attention also should be given to characteristics 3 and 4 listed above. Number 3 says that the paints used for *yūzen* dyeing did not disappear when washed in water, could be used on any silk, and did not ruin the texture of the silk. Also the dyeing of crimson silk, previously impossible due to the blurring of the dyes, became possible as indicated in characteristic 4. The solutions to several other difficult problems in traditional paste-resist dyeing techniques were described in *Yūzen Hiinakata*. Because of this, *yūzen* dyeing received tremendous attention. It should not be forgotten that *yūzen* dyeing was not limited to paste-resist dyeing. In the sixth characteristic listed above, it is suggested that *yūzen* dyeing was applied even to wooden products and that *yūzen* dyeing's primary significance lay in its designs. Soon the technique of *yūzen* dyeing and designs created by Yūzen surpassed all other dyeing methods. *Yūzen* dyeing was recognized as the most superior technique in Kyoto, and the techniques of paste resist gradually were improved as the taste for pictorial designs developed. When the techniques were developed so fully that detailed pictorial expressions of the designs became possible, the term *yūzen* came to signify dyed goods with pictorial designs created by fine lines of paste.

As has been stated at the beginning of this essay, in *yūzen* dyeing today, the outlines of the motifs are resisted in paste. Then various paintings are added, and all of the motifs are paste resisted. Finally the background is dyed by brush painting (*hikizome*). A question arises at this point. While the dyeing of the ground by brush painting is done as a matter of course in today's *yūzen* dyeing, which uses synthetic dyes, it is uncertain whether brush painting was done in the early stages of *yūzen* dyeing. Even among scholars the prevailing notion that *yūzen* dyeing of the ground was done in brush painting has remained fixed and uncontested. In examining examples of *yūzen* dyeing of the past, one must notice that works which were dyed an indigo blue color show conspicuous blurs around the outlines, blurs that are not evident in works dyed in other colors. The blurs would never have occurred had brush painting been used. It is considered that dyeing in indigo blue alone was done by immersion dyeing. Indigo dye, which had always been used in immersion dyeing, had never been suitable for brush painting.

Brush painting might have been possible within a small space in the extant examples, many of which have indigo blue ground or have a large space of indigo blue. In examining those fragments in the Nomura Collection whose ground is dyed indigo blue, researchers have found that the motifs in several fragments are reserved in white by paste resist on the surface but are dyed in indigo blue in the back. If these had been dyed by brush painting, the dye would not have penetrated to the back of the paste-resisted motifs. Apparently the grounds of these materials were dyed by immersion after the paste had been applied on one surface of the material.

Many works with indigo blue background in this exhibition are also considered to have been dyed by immersion. For example, in the *kosode* fragment with curtains, weeping cherry trees, and drying fishnet (No. 32), fine lines of paste that are characteristic to *yūzen* dyeing cannot be recognized in the areas where the indigo blue motifs and motifs in other colors meet. This is because the *yūzen* dyeing was done after the immersion dyeing in indigo had been done. Also, in the *furisode* with curtains, cherry trees, and maples (No. 37), while the motifs inside the curtains are clearly and precisely divided by the white and narrow fine lines of paste, the immersion-dyed outlines of the curtains (the border with the indigo dyed area) and outlines of the cherry trees and maples are blurred.

One can conclude that, even in *yūzen* dyeing, the dyeing of the ground in indigo was done by immersion. In that case the dyeing of the ground should have been the first step in the entire process. The dyeing of the ground of today's *yūzen* dyeing by *hikizome* comes at the end of the dyeing process, after the details of the motifs have been dyed and after the motifs have been resisted in paste. As has been explained previously, the *hikizome* dyeing of the ground became possible after synthetic dyes became available. At present immersion dyeing in *yūzen* dyeing is seldom practiced. The idea that *yūzen* dyeing always is done by *hikizome* has become fixed and left unexamined in the study of the process of immersion dyeing and *yūzen* dyeing.

Until at least the mid-Edo period had not the immersion dyeing normally been completed during the dyeing of the grounds? And were these grounds not only in indigo blue but also in other colors? These questions are raised in studying the first sentence in the above quotation from *Yūzen Hiinakata* which says, "In *yūzen* dyeing favorite motifs are first sketched. Paste is applied, then the ground is tie-dyed in different colors." The blurs of the outlines of the tie-dyed areas are not corrected. Then the painting is done." Here the process of ground dyeing is done first, and the application of the paste is simultaneously done with the tying which is apparently for *shibori* dyeing, i.e. dyeing by immersion. Actually, as in the *kosode* with chrysanthemum branches in bands of No. 40, examples in which the ground dyeing seems to have been done first even in other colors are found. We need to study again and again the processes of *yūzen* dyeing in the premodern age.

As was described in the essay "*Kosode* at the End of the Premodern Age," the *yūzen* dyeing of the early period had a very different connotation from what we know as *yūzen* dyeing today. The *yūzen* dyeing that at one time swept over Japan became obsolete by the onset of the Genroku years. In reading the technical instructions on *yūzen* dyeing in *kosode* fashion books, it is apparent that the number of designs which included *yūzen* technique reduced drastically. For example, in *Wakoku Hiinakata Taizen* (*An Encyclopedia of Japanese Fashion Books*), published in 1698, only nineteen designs among 116 contained in the book were intended to be created by *yūzen* techniques. But *yūzen* dyeing was on the rise again after fifteen years of unpopularity. Forty-six designs out of ninety-six are *yūzen* designs in *Shōtoku Hinagata*, published in 1713, and fifty-five out of 144 are *yūzen* designs in *Hinagata Gionbayashi*, published in 1714.

The *yūzen* which was popular before the Genroku years is not synonymous with today's *yūzen* dyeing. On the other hand the *yūzen* of the second period of popularity can be interpreted as the most similar to today's *yūzen* dyeing. In *yūzen* dyeing designs are expressed very freely as if they were paintings, and subtle nuances of the colors and shades can be attained. It may be redundant to add that these are the reasons for the popularity of *yūzen* dyeing after the eighteenth century. It was in this *yūzen* dyeing that the free pictorial expression, which had been dreamed of and sought after in craft designs since ancient times, was almost completely realized.

The Symmetrical Edozuma *Style*

Yūzen dyeing allows a great deal of freedom in pictorial expression and color. After its introduction, people's tastes in *kosode* design tended increasingly toward *yūzen* dyeing. *Kosode* decorated through the older tradition of *shibori* dyeing and embroidery gradually lost their appeal. The tradition that was born in the Momoyama period and developed into the Keichō and Kanbun styles matured in the Genroku style. However, it suffered a decline after the mid-eighteenth century. Later in the century, *kosode* design underwent a great transformation. The public, saturated with the free and colorful effects of *yūzen* dyeing, began to seek patterned designs once again. Those patterns of the latter half of the Edo period (latter half of the eighteenth century) were called *Edozuma* patterns, and they contained motifs arranged in bilateral symmetry, starting from the lower edge of one side of the neckband, spreading downward to the skirt and then toward the center back line, where they spread upward to the lower edge of the opposite side of the neckband. Bilaterally symmetrical compositions already had been in fashion in the Momoyama period and remained a regular style. But the fashion-setting designs which best reflected the spirit of the era were mostly asymmetrical in composition. The return of symmetry in *Edozuma* can be regarded as an epoch-making turn of events.

The large areas of undecorated space around the waist and upper body of the *Edozuma* style were similar to those of the Kanbun style. But the spaces took on a different significance during the latter half of the eighteenth century. In the Kanbun style a *kosode* was likened to a single canvas. An empty space in a Kanbun design was part of the design filling the area between two motifs, a "not-yet-decorated" space. In the *Edozuma* style, the empty space was considered, from the beginning, the outside area of the canvas, a "nondecorated" space. The canvas area of *Edozuma* extended only from the lower edges of the neckband to the skirt. Within this "frame" motifs were placed continuously along the right edge of the overlap to the left overlap without interruption from the side seam lines or center back seam. The use of small-sized motifs contrasted greatly to the overcrowded and flamboyant motifs characteristic of Genroku style designs. The *Edozuma* style contained fewer motifs on the back of the robe, as the major motifs were located on the front. Until this period the *kosode* design was emphasized on the back of the garment without exception. In the fashion books the posterior view of the *kosode* was the standard display illustration. The focus moved to the front of the kimono when the *Edozuma* style became popular. It may be more accurate to say that the composition in *kosode* design shifted as the perspective of looking at *kosode*, or at the women who wore *kosode*, changed. In any event, peoples' perspective on clothing changed drastically after the mid-eighteenth century.

Certain aspects of the fashion environment at that time are worth noting. Decorative *kosode* were being promoted to the general population and new fashions spread rapidly due to the availability of *kosode* fashion books. The swift coming-and-going of new fashions among so many different people was unprecedented and was contrary to development of fashion in the first half of the premodern period. Then, *yūzen* dyers sought greater flexibility only to exhaust the creative potential of the designs. Bored with superficiality, people began to seek neat, clean designs and ceased to be swayed by the tastes of the times.

A resistance to flamboyant *kosode* most likely prevailed during the first half of the eighteenth century; there were, however, some positive factors leading up to the popularity of standardized designs during the later half of the Edo period. For instance, the birth of new ideas about beauty, such as *iki* and *soko-itari*, took place. *Iki* refers to a spirit that motivates one to keep his feelings and appearance more reserved. *Soko-itari*, an emphatically dramatized form of *iki*, refers to workmanship with which one controls outward beauty and seeks a more hidden beauty. From one point of view, the concepts of *iki* and *soko-itari* were a definite form of resistance, a negative cultural reaction to the excessiveness of the previous culture. The designs produced after many periods and many changes reflected a new, more understated aesthetic.

The Modern Kimono

Ishimura Hayao
Chief Research Worker, Applied Arts Department
National Museum of Modern Art

The Contemporary Kimono Defined

Contemporary kimonos may be classified according to the three primary methods by which they are produced. The first category includes those made with manufactured weave and dye products. The second consists of kimonos made by hand in traditional, small-scale production centers, which have barely survived the premodern age. The third category comprises artistic kimonos produced by kimono "authors," or artists. Examples of handcrafted kimonos made in local production centers include *bingata* and *bashōfu* (abaca cloth) in Okinawa, *Ōshima tsumugi* (pongee) in Amami Ōshima, *yūzen* and weaves in Kyoto, *kenjō hakata* in Fukuoka, *nagasaka chūgata* in the Tokyo area, *kihachijō* in Hachijō Island, *Echigo jōfu* in Niigata, and *yūki tsumugi* (pongee) in Ibaragi. In all parts of Japan, a variety of special traditional techniques used in making handcrafted kimonos have been passed down through the years. In these places handmade kimonos are still produced. The handmade form of Japanese ethnic dress still is reaching the general public, bypassing the kimonos produced by modern manufacturers.

Evidenced by the fact that traditional kimonos are still in demand today, it is clear that the Japanese people's love for these kimonos has deep roots. In the past, kimonos not only were worn for practical purposes but frequently were produced just for beauty's sake. This helps explain why the Japanese still seek handcrafted kimonos today, although they no longer wear kimonos on a daily basis. Today, people usually wear kimonos as formal dress (*haregi*) at school-related entrance and commencement ceremonies, weddings, gatherings for tea and flower arranging ceremonies, and at various parties. According to taste, kimonos that are exceptionally beautiful are required for these gala occasions.

Men have less occasion than women to wear kimonos, and the number of men who do wear them is very small. Men's kimonos for gala occasions are usually black and show little variety. However, it appears that, in premodern cities such as Edo, Ōsaka, and Kyoto, men wore kimonos bearing the gorgeous designs associated with modern women's kimonos. Today, that tradition of elaborately decorated kimonos for men is visible only in the costumes worn in kabuki theaters, at festivals, *bon-odori* (community summer dances), master class recitals of dancing and other private disciplines, and in other kinds of entertainment. Except for these instances, the tradition of elaborately designed kimonos has been preserved only in women's kimonos. For these reasons kimono artists usually apply their talents to women's kimonos. Likewise, only women's kimonos usually are exhibited in kimono exhibitions, which are held frequently.

The Japanese Traditional Craft Exhibition

In 1955, the Cultural Properties Protection Committee (today's Department of Cultural Properties Protection in the Bunkachō) established the annual Japanese Traditional Craft Exhibition, marking the first appearance of the so-called "kimono authors." Seven areas of exhibition were included: ceramic arts, dyeing and weaving, lacquer arts, metalwork, wood and bamboo work, dolls and other arts (including glasswork, cloisonné wear, gems, and ivory work). Participating in the first exhibition were craftsmen from throughout the country who already were actively producing works as individual artists, craftsmen who had gone through apprenticeships under the masters, and craftsmen of the traditional arts. Craftsmen whose works were displayed in the dyeing and weaving area of the first exhibition worked mostly in kimono studios. Others were craftsmen of *obi* belts and *kumihimo* (braided cords). Although exhibitions for the purpose of promoting industries had been held often since the Meiji period (1867–1912), this was the first attempt to have an exhibition of an artistic nature for crafts. The exhibition of traditional crafts was a success and has been held annually since its inception.

The purpose of the Japanese Traditional Craft Exhibition was to provide an active forum for the craftsmen who had studied in the traditions of their own country and showed talent within the classic artistic disciplines, as well as for the craftsmen of the new generation who would follow in their path. This policy is thought to have been enforced as a protective measure against the great changes which occurred in Japanese society as a result of World War II. It was hoped that the Cultural Properties Protection Committee's policy of holding an annual exhibition, implemented ten years after the war, would promote Japanese culture.

The first exhibition left a very strong impression upon the contemporary public. In the following years the craft exhibition grew both in its influence and its size. Even today, the Japanese Traditional Craft Exhibition is the only place where kimonos created by kimono artists are presented to the public in such a format.

Leaders of the Craft Exhibition

When discussing "Japanese crafts," one discovers that there is a great difference between the type of crafts included in the Japanese Traditional Craft Exhibition and those prevalent at Nitten, the location of an important annual series of art exhibitions in the areas of sculpture, Japanese painting, Western-style painting, crafts, and calligraphy. The government-sponsored Nitten exhibition was established during the Meiji period in 1882 and has left sure footprints in Japanese modern arts and crafts. Until the Japanese Traditional Craft Exhibition was originated, the exhibition in Nitten was the most comprehensive representation of Japanese crafts.

Primarily active through Nitten, and recognized as artists by others, were a group of craftsmen who were educated at art schools. Although they were active in dyeing and weaving, their activities in the fields of tapestries and panels (decorations similar to paintings) were limited and they seldom employed the traditions of the kimono. They were part of the Modern Craft Movement, a movement of certain contemporary craftsmen-artists who, after receiving art school education, studied in Europe and were influenced by or sensitive to such movements as Art Nouveau, Art Deco, Bauhaus, William Morris's Craft Movement, and others. These men created crafts with a modernist influence which swayed all the cities, beginning in Tokyo, during the Taishō period (1912–1926). The traditional craftsmen of the traditional studios never thought of themselves as artists, nor did society regard them as such.

In contrast to the artists of the Modern Craft Movement, there were some individuals, even among school-educated crafsmen-artists, who understood and advocated the importance of Japanese traditional crafts. For example, the ceramic artists Hamada Shōji and Tomimoto Kenkichi and a lacquer artist named Matsuda Gonroku learned through traditional techniques and walked their own paths instead of trying to imitate Western-style arts. They sent their works to the Japanese Traditional Craft Exhibition and assumed roles of leadership.

Hamada, Tomimoto, and Matsuda were three of a group of craftsmen who took leadership roles in the early period of the Japanese Traditional Craft Exhibition. This group of craftsmen were not the successors of one particular traditional technique nor were they the type to stay in one studio. Rather, they all shared a common background as well-informed craftsmen-artists who received higher education, traveled to foreign countries, and generally gained a wide breadth of experience. At the same time, they knew best the techniques of the traditional crafts and appreciated their value.

Serizawa Keisuke (1895–1984), a stencil dye (*katazome*) artist, walked the same path of leadership as Hamada and the others. Although he did not submit his works to the exhibition, he served as a screening committee member for the exhibition in its earlier years. He chose the art of *katazome* when he was moved by the crafts theories of Ryū Sōetsu (1889–1916). Rescuing the traditional techniques from the conservative traditional studios, Serizawa established his own style in the early days of his artistic career, which came to be called "Serizawa style." The basis of his *katazome* was a method which he mastered in traditional dyers' shops. He also learned from the *bingata* resist technique of Okinawa.

The modernist craftsmen of Serizawa's time were using new materials and new methods in an attempt to create new expressions in the style of European Modernism. The works by these modernist craftsmen may have appeared to represent the artistic forefront at the time, but on the other hand they fell below the standard of traditional craftsmanship in terms of completeness. The wax-resist (*rō*) dyeing method, imported for its convenience and low cost, is an illuminating example of this. Wax-resist dyeing has never developed to a significant extent in Japan, neither has it appealed to the Japanese people's sense of beauty. Only modernist dye artists have achieved success in the use of wax-resist dyeing, applying it not to kimono production but to "new life style" interior decoration, such as panels and wall hangings.

Serizawa, in contrast to his peers, learned and continued to use the "old" materials and techniques, such as *katazome* with paste resist. The history of Japanese clothing cannot be considered without mention of *katazome*. It can be said that *katazome* is in the blood of the Japanese who design Japanese clothing. Although traditionally *katazome* had been used only in dyeing of clothing, Serizawa applied the *katazome* technique to other aspects of design in addition to kimono dyeing. Still retaining the traditional katazome technique, he created epoch-making designs on both flat surfaces and three-dimensional objects.

Ryū Sōetsu, a disciple of Serizawa, never stopped praising the beauty of everyday things and the beauty of the kimono of the Japanese past. In 1924, Ryū was acquainted with a ceramic artist, Hamada Shōji. Soon, the two men formed a group of artists who shared many of the same values. Ryū led the group by collecting the so-called folk crafts and by writings that espoused their beauty. The active movement started by Ryū and Hamada is known as the Folk Craft Movement. Opposed to the prevalent notion that craftsmen-artists were the creators of beauty, Ryū and his comrades insisted that the objects used in daily life in Japan contained an inherent beauty which craftsmen-artists should seek to retain. In other words, the movement reestablished the Japanese sense of beauty, which had been ignored in modern art history. Hamada, through ceramic art, and Serizawa, through dyeing, proved that the sense of beauty developed by Japanese in the past was very rich indeed.

Nakamura Katsuma (1894–1982), a *yūzen* dyeing artist and a contemporary of Serizawa, became a private pupil of a designer in Tokyo in 1913. At that time, the only design practiced among Japanese contemporary craftsmen-artists had a bilaterally symmetrical composition, with the back line as its axis, as if a single pattern were turned over and the same design repeated to achieve symmetry. What a suffocating composition this was! However, the design plan used during this time was drawn only on the front overlap area of the kimono, and only this design was given to the studios. The technicians in the studios were content to develop this design only in bilateral composition because they worked by piece rate. Although they adapted the new designs created by the painters and designers and used the hand painting *yūzen* technique, they produced kimonos which gave an impression of inferior *katazome* dyeing.

Tokyo, during the early part of the century, was becoming a thriving commercial and industrial center. The demand for new garment designs increased with the city growth. Designers started hiring their own dyeing technicians and producing their own dyed materials. As designers, they knew all too well the dullness of bilateral symmetry in design, and, as soon as designers started to produce their own garments, bilateral symmetry disappeared in Tokyo. The general public finally noticed the anachronistic design. In Kyoto, where not much change had occurred in commerce or industry, the bilaterally symmetrical designs continued to be produced until much later.

Until designers began to produce their own garments, dry goods dealers and other merchants determined kimono designs based on their perception of the current consumer demand. The shift in just who would make the design decisions, consequently, had great impact in the art and business fields. The new producers, understanding the staleness of the current designs, began to produce kimonos based on their own creative ideas. In Tokyo, Nakamura Katsuma was mastering not only the designs but also the practical techniques of dyeing that had belonged to the masters. While doing so, Nakamura noticed that the customers did not show any excitement over the *yūzen* works of the day. He tried to freshen the garment designs by applying the *musenfuse* (no line resist) technique, a simple method of drawing the design with the dyes directly on the material, despite the fact that *musenfuse* was despised by studio technicians as a lower-class technique.

Since his young days, Nakamura had won prizes for his works in design competitions held by dry goods dealers. Later he joined the Mitsukoshi Clothing Store, the most traditional in the field, producing garments for high quality textile fashion shows. During the war, when goods were strictly controlled, he was one of the qualified preservers of the craft techniques who were under the government's special protection. To summarize his life history, he can be called a textile producer of the highest order.

Nakamura, as well as the chief technicians of other traditional *yūzen* studios, had long been subject to the demands of the dry goods dealers and other merchants. But after the war, Nakamura broke away from these commercial restraints. He became a dye artist and sent works to Nikakai and the Japanese Traditional Craft Exhibition. *Katazome* artist Inagaki Nenjirō and *yūzen* artist Kimura Uzan, contemporaries of Nakamura, had similar experiences. All of these men knew that being a dye artist was a totally different experience from just working in the garment production industry. In 1955, when the system of Important Intangible Cultural Assets was made law under the Cultural Properties Protection Act, these craftmen-artists were the first ones to be designated as Possessors of Important Intangible Cultural Assets.

As a result of the efforts and talents of Hamada, Serizawa, Ryū, Nakamura, and other craftsmen-artists, the Japanese Traditional Craft Exhibition grew in stature and popularity. Determining what to include in the exhibition required the skilled opinions of many people. Both kimono artists and scholars in the traditional art fields joined the screening committee. Because of the exhibition's originally modern orientation, works which were traditional were not necessarily considered worthy of exhibition. In addition, it was rather difficult for works produced in the local traditional, professionalized institutions to be accepted in the exhibition. Expressions and techniques which these scholars valued highly crystallized into one distinctive style, called the "traditional craft."

Let us look at persons who first sent their works to the Japanese Traditional Craft Exhibition and thus came to be known as craftsmen-artists. In 1955 Moriguchi Kakō, a technician in a traditional *yūzen* studio, sent his works to the exhibition. He was among the young, talented craftsmen encouraged to send in works by the earlier exhibition committee. His work caused a sensation that is hard for us to imagine today. He won an award of excellence for his kimono titled *Sōshun* (*Early Spring*) in 1955 and received another award the following year. Even today, exhibition-goers who saw Moriguchi's work more than two decades ago exclaim, "It was such a fresh surprise!"

Over thirty exhibitions have been held since the first one in 1955, and the public has gradually gotten used to the style of the works the shows contain. Today's exhibitions of dyed works are familiar and the situation is very different from the time when the exhibition first started, the time when kimonos were considered just local productions having nothing to do with crafts or arts. Many people have forgotten that there was once a time when every job in which traditional techniques and styles were inherited was considered a mere local industry supported by manual labor. The story of Moriguchi's participation in the exhibition is analogous to that of many other participants at that time; the exhibition marked the first wherein the works which craftsmen had been creating were judged correctly as meaningful works of art.

The major characteristics of the Moriguchi works is the *makinori* technique, which can produce a diaper pattern with an effect similar to that of the *nashikoji* (pear ground) lacquer, or sprinkled lacquer. Normally, *yūzen* designs are pictorial, paintings copied on silk ground. In Moriguchi's works, the space for the painting is first created in *makinori*, and the colored decorative ground becomes a profound space. When people first saw the Moriguchi *yūzen* thirty years ago, they may have noticed that mere imitation of painting in the garment design was not interesting enough—the pattern of the kimono had to make a statement of its own.

Moriguchi's skills and talents apparently were discovered and began to bloom when he participated in the first exhibition and won the award for excellence. Up until the exhibition he had dyed virtually any design requested from dealers. After the *makinori* effect in the kimono *Sōshun*—one of three works in different styles he had submitted—was praised at the exhibition, he continued to make works using the *makinori* technique. This technique can be considered to be original to Moriguchi.

Shortly after Shimura Fukumi started learning plant dyeing and weaving from her mother, she sent her works to the exhibition at the encouragement of an acquaintance. Although her works did not extend beyond the amateur level, her sense of color was well received and she was accepted into the exhibition. She received awards over four consecutive years, which prompted the committee to make a new rule that consecutive awards could be given only twice. After two consecutive awards, an artist would receive a special invitation to submit works. Shimura's works were so popular every time they were exhibited that even the screening committee could not resist continuing to give her awards. Her works consist of simple weave *tsumugi* (pongee).

Tsumugi appears to have been woven in any part of Japan where silkworms were kept. In olden days *tsumugi* weaves were rendered to the central government as taxes. During the Edo period (1615–1868) they were produced as merchandise on the demand of the rich townsmen, but *tsumugi* basically were woven for individuals. *Tsumugi*, throughout its long history, always was thought to be an inconspicuous, subdued weave. Decoration of the *tsumugi* fabric was limited to stripes, or ikats. It was natural for people to conclude that no new expression was possible in this common weave, and that *tsumugi* was inflexible when compared to such free designs as the diaper pattern weaves.

The *tsumugi* works that Shimura first submitted to the exhibition must have seemed amateurish compared to those by the other participants, who were mostly professional technicians with long careers in *yūzen*, *katazome*, and other styles. *Tsumugi*, with its precisely calculated stripes and ikats, might have appeared to be the work of a professional except that it may have been too ordinary. Shimura wove the colorful threads that she dyed herself in the way that pleased her; this idea was beyond the imagination of the professional weave technician. Weaves as merchandise were woven according to weave plans, whereas Shimura's works were totally uninhibited.

There is no doubt Shimura's works added an unexpected dimension to the exhibition. By giving Shimura's works consecutive awards, the exhibition proved its purpose. It encouraged the first-rate professional craftsman to publicize his works, thus emphasizing the value of preserving traditional techniques. It also promoted the restoration of crafts in traditional Japanese styles. Although the specific reaction of the general public to Shimura's work is not known, it can be said that, in a sense, the "traditional crafts" were created, in part, with the recognized talents of the young generation.

It is reported somewhere that *katazome* artist Inagaki Nenjirō, as he was looking at some old garments, once questioned: "Why should not there be garments made just for the sake of looking at them?" This notion was not a new one—in fact, contemporary Japanese clothing is a result of the passion of Japanese people's ancestors, who enthusiastically "looked at" what they wore. The kimono artists who have participated in the Japanese Traditional Craft Exhibition are the artists who are perpetuating the power of that tradition.

Chronology

Asuka		552–645
Nara		645–794
Heian		794–1185
Kamakura		1185–1333
Muromachi		1333–1573
Momoyama		1573–1615
	Keichō	1596–1615
Edo		1615–1868
	Early Edo	1615–1688
	Kanbun	1661–1673
	Mid-Edo	1688–1781
	Genroku	1688–1704
	Late Edo	1781–1868
Meiji		1868–1912
Taishō		1912–1926

Catalogue

I Screen with Two *Kosode*

Left:
Kosode fragment with floral motifs
Tsujigahana dyeing
Purple *nerinuki* silk
Momoyama period, late sixteenth to early seventeenth century

In this *tsujigahana* design the floral motifs are reserved white against a purple ground, with the flower petals and leaves in capped (*bōshi*) *shibori* resist and the outlines of the leaves and stems in stitch-resist *shibori*. The whole composition of the original *kosode* cannot be determined with certainty because only a fragment remains today. Probably, it originally had a *chirashi* design, in which units of motifs were distributed quite evenly all over the *kosode*. The design is a simple one, and in some parts the dye is uneven. As explained in an earlier essay in this catalogue, *tsujigahana* design can be divided into these three categories:

1. *Kosode* with comparatively simple compositions and of a naïve taste, in which, probably due to undeveloped skills, there are blurred dye spots.

2. *Kosode* that have closely placed motifs using *shibori* dyeing, with a large portion of freehand ink painting (*kakie*), applied gold or silver leaf (*surihaku*), and embroidery (*nui*). *Kosode* of this category have a colorful and more complicated design.

3. *Kosode* which express a design clearly, freely utilizing a highly developed *shibori* technique, without such additional help as ink painting, and which show a refined although rather one-dimensional design.

This particular *kosode* fragment belongs to the first category. The same design is visible in the portrait of Takeda Shingen, drawn by Hasegawa Tōhaku in 1573, which is preserved in Seikei-in in Wakayama. This fact suggests that the fragment belongs to the earlier *tsujigahana* design. There are other *kosode* fragments in addition to this one with floral motifs reserved white by *shibori* against the background dyed in purple.

45

Kosode fragment with stone pavement and flowers
Tsujigahana dyeing
White *nerinuki* silk
Momoyama period, late sixteenth to early seventeenth century

This *kosode* is mounted on the screen as one piece, but, originally, it was probably not one piece. The lower border of the band with the stone pavement pattern and the upper and lower borders of the flowered band show evidence of having been cut and later seamed together. The upper band with the stone pavement pattern is continuous, with the white background at its upper edge, and it is presumed that the original design was composed in *dan* (divided bands). The present fragment shows a refined design of patterned squares which are rendered clearly in detail, even in the corners, by capped *shibori*. This upper band belongs to the third category of *tsujigahana*.

By contrast, the band with the floral design is characteristic of the second *tsujigahana* category. The blossoms and leaves are rendered in capped *shibori*, with stitch-resist *shibori* defining the flower stems and veins of the leaves; details and shadows are painted in ink. The manner of painting is decorative and a little too formal, but it should be noted that the depiction is based on a detailed study of nature. During its peak, *tsujigahana* design achieved a most realistic depiction of nature through the *shibori* dyeing technique (previously thought to be unfitting for such realistic expression), thereby enlivening the design. There are several examples of *tsujigahana* which are similar to this floral design, such as the famous fragment preserved in Zuisenji. The design of a fragment in the Nezu Museum is very similar to this one and both could have been parts of the same *kosode*. It is interesting that the fragment in the Nezu Museum, like this one, preserves the white background, suggesting that its original design was composed in a *dan* (divided bands) format, as this *kosode* probably was. These two examples, which suggest the design of a whole *kosode*, are very important because most of the extant examples of *tsujigahana* design are only fragments that show motifs.

On the back of this screen there is attached a piece of material with this inscription in black ink: "The third year of Kanbun, Shaku Myosai, the twenty-sixth of March, Hirai Gorobei." The fabric, white *nerinuki* silk, is thought to have been taken from the same material of the band with the stone-pavement pattern or from the band with the floral design. Great caution should be exercised in estimating the date of origin which this

signed fragment implies. However, if the signed fragment can be linked for certain with the *kosode* fragment, it is a significant piece of information which may shed light on the dating of the *tsujigahana* design.

2   *Kosode* Screen with Fans in Allover (*Chirashi*) Design

Tsujigahana dyeing
Asaghi (light blue) *nerinuki* silk
Momoyama period, late sixteenth to early seventeenth century

The ground is dyed in light blue with every design motif in *kanoko* (fawn-dot) *shibori* and *bōshi* (capped) *shibori* resist. After adding more *kanoko shibori* and *bōshi shibori* to the fans and the clouds, which have been reserved in white, these motifs are dyed in *kurobeni* (dark brown) and green while the surrounding areas are resisted. Finally the bones of the fans and veins of the flowers are added by *kakie* (freehand painting). This design belongs in part to both the first and third categories of *tsujigahana* design; however, the cloud motifs are often seen in Keichō-style *kosode*. The blurring by *shibori* indicates that this *kosode* belongs to the later period of *tsujigahana* design, following its peak, rather than the early, undeveloped stage of the technique.

3 Screen in Divided-Background Style with Two *Kosode*

Left:

Kosode fragment with Chinese bellflowers and camellias

Tsujigahana dyeing

Nerinuki silk

Momoyama period, late sixteenth to early seventeenth century

This example of *kosode* belongs to the third category of *tsujigahana* design. It has a refined but colorful design created by dividing the white *nerinuki* silk ground into red and white alternating bands by *somewake* dyeing. The red, light blue, and green camellia branches stand out against the white background, while the white bellflowers are reserved white against the red background. The main characteristic of this example of *tsujigahana* dyeing is that the whole design is executed in *shibori* without any supplementary technique such as painting or applied metallic leaf. It is very difficult to compress the motifs exactly and tighten them with a thick hemp thread to provide the resist in the details, but in this *kosode* the sharp edges and the details of the motifs, such as the corners of the petals and leaves, the stems, and the veins, are rendered clearly through *shibori*. The refined composition and the subdued color organization show the author's deep knowledge of *tsujigahana* design. This *kosode* is thought to have been made after the peak of *tsujigahana*, the late sixteenth to early seventeenth century.

In the red bands, narrow strips of deeper red can be seen. It is thought that the red color is *akane* (madder) and that, originally, the surrounding areas were also in this deeper red. Only the darker parts escaped fading for some reason, and all the other parts faded to yellowish red. There are two other fragmentary examples of this same design in existence and probably they, along with this fragment, are pieces of the same *kosode*. One fragment in the Tōyama Museum in Saitama Prefecture has the same dark red stripes as this *kosode*. The other fragment, which is in the Kyoto National Museum, is more interesting in that it is not just a fragment, but a banner (*hata*) used for decoration of the inside and outside of the sanctuary of the Buddhist temples. The inside of the *hata*, literally "banner," is divided by pieces of material called *tei*. Under these pieces of material the deep red color, probably derived from sappan wood, is revealed. *Tei* are positioned in several places at regular intervals. The intervals and the

width of the *tei* of the banner correspond to the positions and the shapes of the deep red stripes of the *kosode* fragments in the Tōyama Museum and in the Nomura Collection. That means that both of the fragments in the Tōyama Museum and this *kosode* in the Nomura Collection were made into banners at certain points in history.

Because dyed goods and weavings such as silk *kosode* were considered very precious at the time this *kosode* was made, after the owner died, these belongings were donated to the temple where he was buried. The donated *kosode* were remade into such things as temple banners and *uchishiki*, which were used as covers for altars and ceremonial utensils in the temple. Many dyed and woven goods from this historical period remain in these forms. But it is very rare that one piece of *kosode* is preserved partly in the form of a banner, partly as a fragment, and partly in a remade form.

Detail, No. 3

Right:
Kosode with fragment with allover design of flowers and clouds
Shibori, embroidery, and applied gold leaf
Early Edo period, early seventeenth century

The small design of chrysanthemum flowers, dianthus, plums, and pines, which are minutely embroidered in both colored and gold threads are arranged on the black ground of this *kosode*. Although they have all faded away, such minute diaper patterns as the *sayagata* (key fret) pattern, *kikkō* (tortoise shell) motif, *kasumi* (mist) motif, and others covered the black background in gold leaf between the motifs, making this *kosode* "*jinashi*" (no background). The particular category of *kosode* to which this design belongs cannot be determined from this fragment. But the feeling of the design suggests that it could have been a uchikake (a formal outer garment for wear in winter) or *koshimaki* (waist-wrap *kosode*) worn with the summer *kosode* (katabira).

The composition is not simple in its detail; however, because the motifs are evenly and densely distributed over the *kosode*, from a distance it seems as if single motifs merely were repeated. Embroidery is a technique which has great possibilities for executing pictorial designs freely if the time and labor can be devoted unsparingly. But many among the examples of the *nuihaku* (embroidery and applied metallic leaf) technique of the

early premodern period show a design intentionally rendered with a regularity and repetition similar to the pattern of weavings by eschewing the versatility of embroidery. The composition of this design retains the character of the sixteenth century, while the characteristics of the early seventeenth century are visible in the coloring and the use of gold thread and minute gold leaf (*surihaku*). The *nuihaku* technique of the early seventeenth century, first seen in designs like this one, developed into a distinctive technique prevalent during the Keichō style by incorporating into its vocabulary complicated *shibori* techniques.

4   Screen with Two *Kosode*

Left:
Kosode fragment with grapes and lozenges
Tsujigahana dyeing
White *nerinuki* silk
Momoyama period, late sixteenth to early seventeenth century

A *tsujigahana* design of grape motifs and combined lozenges. The areas surrounding the motifs are resisted in *shibori*. The grapes are dyed in light blue, and the leaves are dyed in purple, light blue, and yellow-green colors. The veins of the purple leaves are executed in stitch-resist *shibori*. The outlines of the fruits and of the azure and yellow-green leaves are delineated in black ink; the veins, stems, and vines also are painted in black ink. There are two kinds of lozenge decoration: in one method the lozenges are dyed in purple with *kanoko shibori* and capped *shibori*, and in the other, purple five-petaled blossoms are executed in lozenges by *shibori* against an orange background. The lozenges are rendered precisely, even in the corners, and no distortion is found in the outlines of the five-petaled blossoms. The uncrowded composition of this design is representative of the

4

first category of *tsujigahana* design, but the imprecise delineation of the outlines in ink are characteristic of the second category. The exquisite workmanship of the *shibori*, visible in the *somewake* (divided background) technique of the lozenges, is a quality of the third category, however. Thus the date cannot be determined exactly. The delicate *shibori* technique must date from the peak period of *tsujigahana* design. There is a fragment of the same design preserved in Kyoto which is thought to have belonged to the same *kosode* as this fragment.

Right:
Kosode fragment with fans and floral motifs (Keichō style)
Nuihaku (embroidery and applied gold leaf) and *shibori*
Black *rinzu* (figured satin)
Early Edo period, early seventeenth century

This *nuihaku kosode* apparently was created during the Kanei era in the early Edo period. It contains a major feature of the distinctive *nuihaku* of the early Edo period: mysterious figures neither concrete nor abstract. The complicated *somewake* (divided background) zones in black and white can be read as rolling mountains or cresting waves. The lower borders of these forms have geometric shapes which resemble *mastukawa-bishi* (pine-bark lozenges). Elsewhere in the design, there are roundels paved with *kanoko shibori* and arranged with fan papers that seem to float in the air—perhaps they are *yukiwa* (snow roundels). Minute-scale motifs of flowers, fan papers, and flowing streams are finely embroidered upon these abstract shapes. Also between the motifs, traces of minute patterns in gold leaf (*surihaku*) remain, but almost all have exfoliated. Unlike Momoyama *nuihaku*, the gold leaf does not simply fill in the embroidery but also is used to render such motifs as fan papers, lozenges, mist, and flowing streams against the black background, as well as oaks with diamond-shaped blossoms in the center and pine-bark lozenges against the white background. This *kosode* suggests that the proportion of the *surihaku* (applied gold leaf) used in decoration increased drastically during the Edo period. Today the effect of the *surihaku* is indistinguishable. The original design, which was covered with brilliant gold leaf, must have had a totally different look, one of mystery and beauty, which cannot be gleaned from the subdued expression of the extant fragment.

5   *Kosode* Screen in Divided-Background Style with Wisteria
and Flowers (Keichō Style)

Nuihaku (applied gold leaf and embroidery) and *shibori*

Rinzu (figured satin)

Late Momoyama to early Edo period, early seventeenth century

This is a typical example of the Keichō style. The background is dyed
crimson, black, white, and light blue with complicated and abstract
shapes by *somewake* technique in *shibori*. Embroidery and *surihaku*
(applied gold and silver leaf) are added. The *surihaku* have disappeared
almost completely. Originally, gold and silver leaf of the *kasumi* (mist)
motifs and *sayagata* (key-fret patterns) were applied to the black ground,
with combined floral patterns on the light blue area. The *shippō tsunagi*
(seven treasures) and *kikkō* (tortoise-shell) motifs also filled the crimson
area. The *somewake* of the top area shows a strange configuration resembling a cloud shape. The *yukiwa* (snow roundels) and mountain shapes in
the middle area intricately intertwine. The concrete motifs of wisteria,
cherry blossoms, flowing water, and water weeds, as well as the geometric
motifs of *shippō tsunagi* and *kikkō*, coexist throughout the *kosode*. The
fragments are arranged in the form of a *kosode* and pasted onto the
screen. The continuity of the motifs is quite different from that of the
original *kosode*, but the overall atmosphere and the complexity particular
to the Keichō style still are communicated. It is not easy to date this work,
but, because the design has no central motif, it seems to be an early example of the Keichō style.

5

6   *Kosode* Screen in Divided-Background Style with Pine Boughs, Wisteria, and Flowers (Keichō Style)

Nuihaku (applied gold and silver leaf and embroidery) and *shibori*
Rinzu (figured satin)
Momoyama to early Edo period, early seventeenth century

Many *kosode* were made during the Keichō era (1596–1615) which fore-shadowed the designs of the Kanbun style which followed. In this example, for instance, *somewake* areas in crimson, black, and white depict not simple abstract forms but the concrete forms of pines and flowers. In addition, the contrast between the ground and motifs which became less clear later shows the author's understanding of the *kosode* as a canvas. The rendering of large concrete motifs, characteristic to the Kanbun style, is already recognizable in the Keichō style, which means that these styles followed each other consecutively. The larger area of *kanoko shibori* also is characteristic of the Kanbun style. The *surihaku* peculiar to the Keichō style almost entirely has faded, probably because the *kosode* was washed. Gold-leaf *surihaku* is recognizable on the veins inside the leaf shapes around the waist. *Surihaku* zigzags across the black upper area. *Surihaku* in the floral patterns is applied around the wisteria blossoms on the crimson ground. Plant motifs of wisteria, cherry blossoms, pines, clematis, pinks, and chrysanthemums are beautifully embroidered as are the auspicious motifs of cranes and turtles, suggesting that this *kosode* may have been created as a wedding garment.

6

7   *Kosode* with Waterfall and Footed Tray (Pre-Kanbun Style)

Nuihaku (embroidery and gold leaf) *shibori*
White *rinzu* (figured satin)
Height: 153 cm.; *yuki* (the length from the center back to the sleeve
opening): 62 cm.; sleeve length: 45 cm.; sleeve width: 27.5 cm.
Early half Edo period, mid-seventeenth century

On the back of the garment, water flows out of the rocks and into a
heron-footed water tray below; on the front, water pours into a bamboo
rattan. The motifs are contrastingly dyed (*somewake*), with the outlines of
the footed water tray, rocks, and rattan in black and the flowing water in
saffron yellow stitch-resist *shibori*. The areas that are dyed black are in
resist by *kanoko shibori*, densely placed small white dots strengthening
the decorative effect. Although much of it has disappeared, gold leaf
(*surihaku*) was used throughout much of this *kosode*. Lines painted in ink
are visible in the running water and water drops; these lines are not
"touch-up" brush painting, but the underdrawings on which the gold leaf
was to be laid. Originally, gold leaf was applied both on the outlines of
the motifs and on all the painted lines.

On the upper side of the right sleeve, a fishnet pattern can be seen; this
fishnet pattern was scattered all over the original *kosode*. The occasional
embroidered chrysanthemum flower is thought to be a later addition,
judging by the threads and the embroidery technique used. This *kosode* is
rare in that, originally, it probably was decorated only by *shibori* dyeing
and *surihaku*. The dynamic composition of the design, with its central
focus on the right shoulder emphasizing the clear contrast with the
ground, recalls the Kanbun style, which flourished in the latter half of the
seventeenth century. For example, there is a design very similar to this
kosode recorded in the *kosode* style book *On Hiinakata*, published in
1666. But the technique used to depict concrete motifs by *shibori* is very
close to that of *tsujigahana*, and the gold leaf which covered whole areas
of the original *kosode* suggests a relationship with *jinashi* (no background) *kosode*. In conclusion, this *kosode* incorporated at an early date
the design concepts of the Kanbun style while still preserving many characteristics of the Momoyama to early Edo style. For these reasons this
kosode should be placed historically at the transitional stage from *nuihaku* of the early Edo period, represented by Keichō style, to the Kanbun

style. It is apparent from the awkward continuity of the motifs that this *kosode* was remade in later years. Both the width and the length of the kimono were shortened, and the sleeves suggest that they were recut from *furisode*.

8   *Kosode* with Plum Trees (Kanbun Style)

Shibori and embroidery
White *rinzu* (figured satin)
Height: 141 cm.; *yuki*: 64 cm.; sleeve length: 50 cm.; sleeve width: 32.5 cm.
Early half Edo period, latter half seventeenth century

Large plum tree branches boldly extend toward the left sleeve and down the skirt in a central design focused on the upper right sleeve. The big branches are executed in crimson and indigo *kanoko shibori* and stitch-resist *shibori*. Around these branches, plum blossoms and small twigs are embroidered with crimson, purple, light green, and other colored threads as well as gold threads. Many *kosode* in the Kanbun style display a composition similar to this one, in which the major motif is suspended from a shoulder to the skirt area.

One can imagine the large size of the branches, which is implied by the depiction of only parts of the motif. This composition recalls a common design from the painting *Rōbai-zu* (*An Old Plum Tree*) drawn by Kanō Sansetsu and preserved in The Metropolitan Museum of Art in New York. However, the feeling of the two works differs. Conspicuous joint seams and later additions in some parts of the material are the result of the remaking of the *kosode* in later years from material inherited in the form of *uchishiki* (fragments for temple use).

8

9   *Kosode* Screen with Fans and Circled Characters

Shibori and embroidery
White *nume* (satin)
Early half Edo period, late seventeenth century

The white satin (*nume*) is dyed in *somewake* (divided background), in crimson and indigo blue in *kanoko shibori*, and in black with iron mordant. The radiate bones of the large fans are embroidered in gold *koma* stitch; inside, the fans are filled with embroidered clematis and vine scroll (*karakusa*) patterns. Around the fans, a series of circular patterns containing Chinese characters are embroidered with colored and gold threads. They include *raku* (to fall), *kaku* (crane), *hai* (wine cup), *chū* (inside), *go* (five), *rō* (old), *hō* (cliff), *man* (ten thousand), *sai* (years), *sen* (thousand), and *nen* (years). The characters suggest a poem, "A Crane," by Haḳu Raku Ten recorded in *Wakan Rōeishū* (*Anthology of Japanese and Chinese Poems*):

Kijō ni	*A voice is heard from above*
koe kitari	As I lie on a pillow;
sen-nenzuru	In the wine cup
haichū ni	A thousand-year-old crane
kageotosu	Reflects its shadow
Gorōhō	On the summit of Gorōhō

The way in which the clematis and vine-scroll patterns are sewn and compressed within the fans recalls the Keichō style. On the other hand, *kanoko* dots, which are rather big in size and densely distributed, are characteristic of the Genroku style. The composition in which the large fans become the central motifs of the design apparently belongs to the Kanbun style. The details, however, are closely packed with motifs and patterns. It seems most likely that the *kosode* dates to the very last years of the Kanbun style and very close to the beginning of the Genroku style.

9

10

Kosode Screen in Horizontal Bands Style with Paulownia and
Snow Roundels

Shibori and embroidery
Saffron yellow *nume* (satin)
Early to mid-Edo period, mid-seventeenth to early eighteenth century

---

The ground is composed of *dangawari* (alternating horizontal bands) with
paulownia patterns on every other band, with magnified snow roundels
(*yukiwa*) over the background. Inside the snow roundels cranes, turtles,
and poems are embroidered. These snow roundels are dyed in crimson,
indigo blue, and black *kanoko shibori* and in black stitch *shibori* with
iron mordant. The outlines are defined by brush painting. The *kanoko*
dots are small and evenly sized, suggesting a highly advanced technique.
The shapes of the cranes, turtles, and young pines are traced by the *kanoko shibori*, and, inside, the outlines of these shapes are embroidered.

The color of the ground is light brown only because it is dirty; originally,
judging by the remnant in the Nomura Collection, it was bright saffron
yellow. The large motifs and the abundant use of gold threads applied to
the characters, paulownia patterns, and the borderlines of the *dangawari*
fall within the Kanbun style. However, the consistent rendering of the
design and the ordered composition are characteristics of the mid-Edo
period. Therefore, this work belongs either to the last phase of the
Kanbun style or the early Genroku style. The poem in the snow roundel
at top, a song of celebration by the former Dainagon Tameie, is recorded
in *Zokujūi Wakashū* (*Volume Two: Anthology of Poems*):

Ikemizu no	Your majesty's reign
taezu	is always clear as water
miyo	in the pond; it will last
matsu no	for a thousand years, even
towani	forever, like the pine trees.

The other poem, in the lower snow roundel, is a winter song by the for-

mer Dainagon Tameyo and is recorded in *Shin Senzai Wakashū* (*The New Anthology of a Thousand Poems*):

Hisakata no.	Your reign grows without limit
sora ni	Like the snow which
miyuru	accumulates on the pines
kitakaki	on the mountain tops reaching
matsu no	toward the sky.

Both poems celebrate a prosperous and peaceful society. From the auspicious motifs of cranes, turtles, young pines, and paulownia it appears that this *kosode* was made with good wishes for future happiness; it probably was worn for a wedding.

11   *Kosode* with Frames (Kanbun Style)

Shibori and embroidery
Yellow *rinzu* (figured satin)
Height: 157 cm.; *yuki*: 61.5 cm.; sleeve length: 42 cm.; sleeve width: 31.5 cm.
Early Edo period, circa late seventeenth century

Comparatively large frames are scattered throughout this design, whose focus is on the upper back. The ground is dyed in *somewake* in saffron yellow while the motifs are resisted in capped *shibori*, and the outlines of the frames and the letters were dyed in black and indigo blue by *kanoko shibori*. The motifs were touched up with a paint brush at the time the dye was squeezed out of the garment, and hidden stitches embroidered in

gold and color were added. In the frames, which are reserved in white, embroidered motifs of plums, chrysanthemums, and cherry blossoms are plentiful.

Kosode with frame motifs frequently are found in genre paintings of the early Edo period. Also, many examples containing frame motifs are recorded in *kosode* fashion books of the late seventeenth century. This indicates that the frames were one of the fashionable motifs of the early Edo period.

The unnatural sequence of motifs suggests that this *kosode* was remade extensively in a later period. Except for the fact that the sleeves have been shortened and the neckbands and *okumi* (overlaps) added, there are no missing parts to the *kosode*. Even so, its design is inharmonious and the composition of the empty areas is awkward. It is hard to understand why the author left the inside of some of the frames undyed. In addition, it is very mysterious that a darker color zone appears on some parts of the skirt, and that on the dividing lines of the two color zones a series of holes made by needles, probably for *shibori*, are recognizable. While no conclusive evidence exists, this *kosode* may have been left incomplete.

12   *Kosode* with Scattered Flutes (Kanbun Style)

Shibori
Rustic gold *rinzu* (figured satin)
Height: 138 cm.; *yuki*: 63 cm.; sleeve length: 39 cm.; sleeve width: 26 cm.
Early Edo period, circa late seventeenth century

The "scattered design" (*chirashi*) of flutes is in *somewake* (divided dye) of navy blue, light blue, rustic gold, and black, with partial ink paintings on the outlines. Evident are both *kanoko shibori* and another *shibori* technique to resist the surrounding areas of the motifs. Hemp threads remain

in some surrounding areas of *shibori*, recalling its connection with the *tsujigahana*; however, the exacting technique of *shibori* and the expressiveness of *tsujigahana* have already been lost. From the composition, this *kosode* is thought to have been made in the latter part of the seventeenth century, but there is still room for study; a quick answer cannot be given at this point. This *kosode* was remade extensively in later years, and the sleeves and the skirt were shortened.

13 *Kosode* with Chrysanthemum Bush (Kanbun Style)

Shibori and embroidery
White *rinzu* (figured satin)
Height: 137.5 cm.; *yuki*: 58 cm.; sleeve length: 34 cm.; sleeve width: 29.5 cm.
Early half Edo period, latter half of the seventeenth century

This is another example of the Kanbun style of composition in which the central design is focused on the right part of the body, especially around the shoulder area. The chrysanthemum blossoms are combined with cloud shapes using *shibori* dyeing. Chrysanthemums and pink dianthus surround these motifs. The chrysanthemum blossoms are executed in indigo and crimson *kanoko shibori* and stitch-resist *shibori*. The floral motifs are embroidered in light green, crimson, and white colored threads, with gold threads added. The atmosphere of this design is very similar to that of the *kosode* fragment with chrysanthemums and *magaki* fence (No. 31). This is thought to have been created in the later half of the seventeenth century. Dirt and damaged sections are clearly visible in this *kosode*, and the incontinuity of the motifs is visible in places. It appears that this *kosode* was once disassembled for more practical uses, such as *uchishiki* (temple cloths). Sometime later, others attempted to reproduce the original garment's design as closely as possible.

13

Kosode with Plum Trees (Genroku Style)

Embroidery and *shibori*
Purple *rinzu* (figured satin)
Height: 145 cm.; *yuki*: 62.5 cm.; sleeve length: 42 cm.; sleeve width: 31 cm.
Mid-Edo period, early eighteenth century

This is a typical Genroku-style *kosode*. The design consists of geometrically rendered bamboo motifs, which spread in concentric circles from the
left shoulder to the skirt, and the plum tree motif, which rises from the
skirt to the shoulders in one big curve topped with snow, represented by
magnified semicircular motifs. The technique used is mostly *kanoko shibori*
on purple ground; on the back right side, snow motifs float against the
indigo dyed ground. When the ground was dyed purple, the snow motif
was reserved in white by capped *shibori* and later dyed in indigo by resisting the surrounding areas in *kanoko shibori*. The plum blossoms are reserved
in white by capped *shibori*, and most of the blossoms have hidden outlines embroidered with yellow-green threads.

Other blossoms have stamens and petals painted in ink. The ink lines may
look like *kakie* touch-up painting, but are the underlining for the embroidery, evidenced by the needle holes left along the ink line. The trunk and
branches of the plum tree are embroidered in *tsukuroi* (darning) stitch and
norikake stitch with yellow-green threads, and the small plum blossoms
and branches are embroidered in *kinkoma* stitch. The *kanoko shibori* has
far larger dots compared to the ones in the earlier Edo period and they are
even in size, characteristic of the Genroku-style *kanoko shibori*. It is
apparent by the clear division between the indigo blue and the purple
zones in *shibori* that a highly advanced technique of *shibori* was used to
make this *kosode*.

The semicircular snow motif, called *setsurin* (snow ring), is one of a number of frequently appearing motifs in Japanese dyeing and weaving design.
The combination of *setsurin* and plum tree reminds the viewer of the
appearance of a pine tree with its needles blown by the wind. A combined
design of pine, bamboo, and plum is called *shō-chiku-bai*, and in Japan it
has been a most familiar and beloved motif. In olden times especially, '
Japanese loved metaphoric designs such as this one, alluding to an auspicious purpose for this design by intertwining the image of the pine tree

with the skillful rendering of the plum and bamboo. This kind of mystery-solving design was in fashion particularly from the early seventeenth to the early eighteenth century.

15   *Kosode* with Flowers, Rafts, and Stream (Genroku Style)

Embroidery and *shibori*
White *rinzu* (figured satin)
Height: 148.5 cm.; *yuki*: 59.5 cm.; sleeve length: 42 cm.; sleeve width: 30 cm.
Mid-Edo period, early part of the eighteenth century

The chrysanthemums over the raft and over the waves first are reserved white by capped *shibori*, and then embroidered. The rounded chrysanthemums are embroidered in hidden stitch with crimson threads, of which some parts are damaged, exposing the ink underlines. The stems are embroidered with *matoi* (twining) stitch in yellow-green, and the leaves and blossoms facing the sides are in golden *koma* stitch, as are the crests of the waves. The rafts, which are one of the major motifs of the design, are dyed in crimson and indigo blue. The other major motif, the stream, is dyed in indigo blue. These motifs are dyed by the authentic *kanoko shibori* technique and the surrounding areas of the *shibori* are corrected in hand brush painting. The *kanoko* dots are quite large and even in size, and the composition of the whole design is characteristic of the Genroku style as is No. 14. In composition and coloring, this *kosode* also is similar to No. 16, and these two works seem to date from the same period.

This *kosode* was disassembled once and resewn in later years to form a kimono, at which point the sleeves were shortened. Consequently, the discontinuity of the motifs is visible especially on the neckbands and front of the *kosode*.

15

16   *Kosode* with Chrysanthemums, Waterfall, and Characters (Genroku Style)

Embroidery and *shibori*
White *rinzu* (figured satin)
Height: 153 cm.; *yuki*: 63 cm.; sleeve length: 45 cm.; sleeve width: 31 cm.
Mid-Edo period, early half eighteenth century

In accordance with the typical Genroku style, this design contains large chrysanthemum leaves and a stream. The combination of chrysanthemums and water is a decorating motif frequently used since the Kamakura period as a sign for long life. The chrysanthemum flowers are embroidered with gold and colored threads. There are two ways to depict chrysanthemum leaves. In the first method the leaves are dyed in ink and the outlines embroidered in hidden stitch with colored and gold threads. The veins of the leaves are embroidered also with the same threads and with gold threads in *koma* stitch. The second method involves dyeing the leaves gray by *kanoko shibori*. The surrounding areas of *shibori* are hand painted to clarify the outlines of the leaves, while the veins of the leaves are dyed in black with a brush. The water is rendered geometrically with simple indigo blue dye and lines of the *kanoko* dots.

Some blurring is seen in the indigo blue areas. The blurring occurred when the water was dyed in *shibori*, its surrounding areas kept in resist, as indicated by the needle holes remaining around the flowing-water motifs. The outlines were touched up also by hand painting after the *shibori* was completed. Authentic *kanoko shibori* was applied to the gray areas and the outlines were corrected by hand painting.

The indigo areas with yellow *kanoko* design are created by a technique called *surihitta*. *Surihitta* produces a dotted *kanoko* effect through a stenciled pattern, with pigments or paints applied to the pattern with a brush. *Kanoko* was one of the most loved designs in Japan, but authentic *kanoko* was subject to the sumptuary law of 1683 since the technique was time-consuming and therefore costly. *Surihitta* was invented as a substitute for *kanoko shibori*.

The character motifs extending from the right sleeve to the left are produced through *surihitta*. These Chinese characters read from left as follows: *shin* (deep), *en* (glamour), *nō* (thick). The same letters extend from the left

sleeve to the right chest on the front of the *kosode*. These characters most certainly were taken from a poem, but the source has not been identified. To use Chinese characters as a *kosode* motif was very popular from the mid- to late seventeenth century, but that fashion was outdated by the end of the seventeenth century, or the Genroku era. Despite the letter motifs the design of this *kosode* is typical of the Genroku style, as was indicated earlier. The garment probably dates from the beginning of the eighteenth century.

The lower part of the front right sleeve, the edge of the left overlap, the entire right overlap, and the tip of the right neckband are later additions. The shoulders are sewn together, although usually a single piece of material was used for the front and back of the *kosode*. The sleeves also are shortened.

17 Screen with Two *Kosode*

Left:
Kosode fragment with bamboo hedge, chrysanthemums, and characters
Dye and embroidery
White *rinzu* (figured satin)
Mid-Edo period, early half eighteenth century

Over the background of bamboo hedge, large character motifs stand out. *Karamatsu* (larch) motifs decorate the hedge in *chirashi* (scattered) design. The letters, *sensai* (a thousand years), are in gold brocade with a diaper pattern of peonies and vine scrolls, which are appliquéd to the ground. It may take a moment to recognize the 3- to 4-centimeter-long stripes, whose colors have faded. Like the *kosode* fragment with bellflowers and camellias (No. 3, left) this fragment was once made into a banner, and the

striped areas are thought to have been hidden under other fragments. *Karamatsu* motifs are embroidered in colored and gold threads. The hedge is dyed in *shibori* immersion dyeing in indigo blue and yellow to develop a green color. The blurred outlines of the hedge are corrected.

Detail, No. 17

Right:

Kosode fragment in divided-background style with bamboo hedge and characters

Dye and *shibori*

Chirimen (crepe)

Mid-Edo period, first half eighteenth century

Similar to the design of the *kosode* fragment at left, this fragment contains a diagonally woven bamboo hedge and large letters. The crimson *somewake* (divided background) is achieved by *shibori* dyeing. The letters read *wakatake* (young bamboo). The letter *waka* ("young") is executed in crimson *kanoko shibori*, and the letter *take* ("bamboo") is in indigo *kanoko shibori*. The central cream-colored part of the hedge is dyed first. Then it is dyed in indigo blue, probably with *airō* (indigo wax), and yellow after the paste has been applied. Major motifs of large letters often are seen in Kanbun-style *kosode*; they went out of fashion in the eighteenth century. A dyeing technique very close to that of *yūzen* dyeing is used in this *kosode*, indicating that it was made during the Genroku period, although the design was old-fashioned at that time.

18   *Kosode* with Wild Oranges, Japanese Larches, and Plums

Shibori and embroidery
Crimson *rinzu* (figured satin)
Height: 146 cm.; *yuki*: 64.5 cm.; sleeve length: 56 cm.; sleeve width: 31.5 cm.
Mid-Edo period, early half eighteenth century

Fig. 1

Against the background of a willow tree, wild oranges and wisteria blossoms are distributed in the area from the waist to the skirt; plum and Japanese larch blossoms are scattered from the waist to the shoulders. The larch motifs resemble chrysanthemums, but they have three circles in the center, whereas chrysanthemum motifs have just one circle or blossom shape in the center. The motifs are resisted in *kanoko shibori* and capped *shibori*, and the ground is dyed in crimson. The stamens of the wild orange and larch blossoms are embroidered in navy blue and crimson in hidden stitch. The orange and plum branches are executed with yellow-green twining (*matoi*) stitch. The petals of the orange blossoms, the central areas of the larch blossoms, and the plum flower buds are decorated with gold *koma* stitch. The bigger, evenly sized *kanoko* dots are typical of the Genroku period. Although the whole composition is based on the Genroku style, in comparison with the most representative works of the Genroku style, such as Nos. 15–17, the separation of the designs into upper and lower areas, divided at the waistline, is more apparent. The separation was influenced by the gradual widening of *obi* sashes from the Genroku period on. Increasing numbers of designs divided at the waistline are found in the *kosode* fashion books of the early eighteenth century.

The discontinuation of motif between the body and the sleeves indicates that this *kosode* was remade in later years, with the sleeves sewn to the wrong sides. Approximately 20 centimeters of the top shoulder line has been removed. Originally this kimono had at least a 75-centimeter sleeve. Figure 1 shows the restored position of the sleeves.

18

19   *Kosode* with Boats, Maples, and Plovers

Embroidery, *yūzen* dyeing, and *surihitta*
White *chirimen* (crepe)
Height: 150 cm.; *yuki*: 61 cm.; sleeve length: 40 cm.; sleeve width: 30 cm.
Mid-Edo period, early eighteenth century

The boat motifs are connected and positioned in four rows. Plovers are situated in the area above the first row, which covers the shoulders; in other areas maple leaves are evenly distributed. The technique applied is primarily *surihitta* (stenciled *kanoko* pattern) in crimson (probably rouge) and indigo blue (indigo wax). The design is brightened by embroidery with crimson, purple, yellow-green, and gold threads. The yūzen technique is applied to the light blue areas by drawing a thin line of paste with a tube for resist dyeing. This *kosode* also was remade in later years. A line of stain is visible on a spot approximately 4.5 centimeters off the front shoulder top. The motifs are separated by this line, which proves that this was the original shoulder line.

19

20　　*Kosode* with Palisade and Camellia Trees (Genroku Style)

Embroidery and *surihitta*

White *rinzu* (figured satin)

Height: 153 cm.; *yuki*: 58 cm.; sleeve length: 46 cm.; sleeve width: 29 cm.

Mid-Edo period, early half eighteenth century

The palisade forms a triangle shape from the skirt to the areas above the waist, on the back, toward the right side. Camellia trees with large, full blossoms are positioned from the skirt to the shoulders and both sleeves. *Surihitta* and embroidery are the main techniques used to create this design. The composition follows the Genroku style in that the left waist area was left undecorated and the focus was placed on just one side of the *kosode*. In the basic Genroku style, which developed from the Kanbun style, motifs are scattered all over the *kosode*, limiting the amount of undecorated space. The composition is stable in spite of the asymmetry. This *kosode* must date from the later Genroku period, when the separation of the design at the waistline was more deliberate, because of the increase in the width of the *obi*, as seen in No. 18. If the viewer looks closely enough, he will see what appears to be one camellia tree, but the design actually consists of two trees separated by the sides.

The trunks of the camellias are dyed in yellow, and indigo blue *surihitta* is placed over them, a combination seen frequently in *kosode* of this period. Exactly what type of yellow dye was used is not clear. If it had been *kariyasu* (miscanthus), it would have been brush painted on the material, which was heated from below to settle the dye. Most camellia blossoms and leaves are dyed either in indigo blue or a light rust color by *surihitta*. The variation of color is attained by embroidering camellia blossoms without *surihitta*, with crimson and purple color threads in hidden stitch, and by scattering flowers embroidered in gold hidden stitch (with petals painted in ink). Buds embroidered in gold *koma* stitch, crimson satin stitch, and yellow green *matoi* (twining) stitch also are visible in some areas.

Originally, indigo blue itself was a dye used in vat dyeing (*tsukezome*). But *airō*, created from indigo, is used as a pigment. *Airō* is made by water-diluting the indigo ingredients collected from the indigo-dyed remnants. After skimming the bubbles of oxidized indigo from the water-diluted dye forty to fifty times, the dye is boiled down into a stick-type applicator. The

applied indigo pigment is called *airō*. The indigo blue used in *surihitta* is derived from *airō*, and the palisade motif of this kimono is probably done with *airō* also. The light rust-color *surihitta* is thought to have been made with another pigment, thinned rouge. Both pigments frequently appear in *surihitta*. *Surihitta* came into fashion in place of hand-sewn *kanoko*, or *hitta shibori*, which was subject to the sumptuary law in the Tenna era. The greatest advantage of *surihitta* lay in the fact that it could be produced less expensively and in larger quantities than authentic *hitta*. For that reason, even after the sumptuary law was relaxed, *surihitta* still was used widely in response to public demand for decorated *kosode*. Another reason for its popularity was that *surihitta*'s plain, ordered effect appealed to the taste of that period.

21 *Kosode* with Chrysanthemums Against a Bamboo Fence (Genroku Style)

Shibori, embroidery, and dye
White *chirimen* (crepe)
Height: 149 cm.; *yuki*: 65 cm.; sleeve length: 44 cm.; sleeve width: 32 cm.
Mid-Edo period, early eighteenth century

The checked pattern, probably dyed with *airō* (indigo wax), represents a rough-woven bamboo fence (*magaki*), against which *surihitta* chrysanthemums dyed by *bengara* (Indian red) are elegantly arranged. The stems of chrysanthemums are embroidered with yellow-green threads in *matoi* (twining) stitch. The black chrysanthemums are dyed in ink and their outlines are embroidered in gold *koma* stitch. The green blossoms are dyed in capped *shibori* and the surrounding areas of *shibori* are covered with crimson embroidery. The arrangement of chrysanthemums against a fence that fills, in an even manner, almost the entire surface of the *kosode* con-

stitutes a composition that conforms to the tradition of the Kanbun style, in which the left side is left blank, with the focus extending from the skirt to the right side of the body, lending a sense of flow toward the left sleeve. But the design of this *kosode* has lost the boldness that was characteristic of the Kanbun style. The formal rendering of chrysanthemums and the orderliness of the composition, similar to No. 20, suggest the taste of the late Genroku to Kyoho periods.

22   *Kosode* with Peonies

Surihitta, kanoko shibori, and embroidery
White *rinzu* (figured satin)
Height: 159 cm.; *yuki*: 63 cm.; sleeve length: 44.5 cm.; sleeve width: 30.5 cm.
Mid-Edo period, early eighteenth century

It has been stated previously that, during this period, the separation of the design above and below the waistline was consciously sought due to the widening of the *obi*. At this transitional point, designs appeared that repeated similar motifs from the skirt to the shoulders. This *kosode* is one example. The composition is in accordance with the Genroku style, in which the even distribution of the motifs was emphasized. It has already lost the characteristics of the Kanbun style. The comparatively large peonies are embroidered in crimson hidden stitch or rendered by *surihitta* with *bengara* (Indian red) and *airō* (indigo wax), while the stems, leaves, and buds are depicted in gold *koma* stitch. In the background of the peonies, from the shoulders to the skirt, there are motifs intended to imitate a waterfall against the navy blue ground. These streamlike motifs, dyed by authentic *kanoko shibori*, probably signify the grains of the wood of a fence, over which peonies bloom in profusion. The upper part of this fence motif is crimson *surihitta* with *bengara*, and its outlines are embroi-

dered with thicker, yellow-green threads. The exactly calculated distribution of the motifs and the intellectualized composition display the creator's expertise in *kosode* design. But the fact that the depiction itself is formalized validates the theory that this *kosode* design dates to the last period of Genroku style.

23   *Kosode* with Japanese Larch Trees and *Koto* (Genroku style)
Dye, embroidery, and *surihitta*
Light blue *rinzu* (figured satin)
Height: 135 cm.; *yuki*: 59.5 cm.; sleeve length: 41.5 cm.; sleeve width: 29.5cm.
Mid-Edo period, early half eighteenth century

Japanese larches rise from the skirt to the shoulders, while the *koto* (Japanese harps) are arranged in a zigzag pattern alongside the trees. The *koto* appear to be of the six-stringed variety. *Surihitta* and embroidery are used to execute this design. First, the motifs are paste resisted and the ground is dyed in light blue. The trunks and the branches of the Japanese larch trees, as well as portions of the Japanese larch trees, are decorated with horse-chestnut *surihitta*, probably using thinned Indian red. Other parts of the Japanese larch trees and the sides of the *koto*, first dyed yellow, are decorated with indigo blue *surihitta*. The wheel-pines and *koto* are embroidered in crimson, light green, and gold in hidden, satin, and *koma* stitch. The outlines of the Japanese larch motifs that have no embroidery are delineated by indigo blue painting. The rhythmic composition from the skirt to the shoulders is similar to that of No. 22. It also resembles a design entitled "A Design with *Koto* and Pine Needles" recorded in the *kosode* fashion book *Nishikawa Hinagata*, published in 1718. It is late Genroku style and is thought to date from the second quarter of the eigh-

teenth century. Because of stains, it was remade in later years, and, therefore, the *kosode*'s original shoulder lines were about 15 centimeters below
the present front shoulder lines. Before these alterations were made, the
original height probably was at least 150 centimeters. The sleeves also
seem to have been shortened indicating that the original was most likely a
long-sleeved *furisode* style.

24   *Kosode* with Weeping Cherry Tree and Flower Hats

Shibori, dyeing, and embroidery
White *nume* silk
Height: 155 cm.; *yuki*: 60 cm.; sleeve length: 48 cm.; sleeve width: 30 cm.
Mid-Edo period, mid-eighteenth century

Branches of a weeping cherry tree spread over the whole surface of this
kosode. Against the cherry blossoms in full bloom, large *ichime* (towns-
women's) hats are scattered. The *ichime* hats are dyed black in ink, and
then embroidered in hidden stitch with crimson threads. Inside the hats
plant motifs such as larches (*karamatsu*) are densely embroidered in gold,
crimson, and blue colored threads. The stems and leaves of the weeping
cherry tree are also embroidered in the same crimson and blue colored
threads by *matsui* and *wari* stitches. Gold *koma* stitch is added to some
parts of the cherry blossoms. At a glance the navy blue and reddish brown
blossoms appear to be *surihitta* (stenciled). But in the surrounding areas
blurred spots which are characteristic of *shibori* dyeing are recognized.
Thus it is supposed that these motifs are first created by the tie dyeing of
the *shibori* technique, painted, and then their outlines are delineated. The
evenly and densely dispersed motifs and the rhythmic composition of the
motifs from the shoulders to the skirt are characteristics shared with such
contemporary examples as Nos. 22 and 23.

24

25   *Kosode* with Storybooks and Characters

Shibori and embroidery
White *nume* satin
Height: 152 cm.; *yuki:* 57 cm.; sleeve length: 46 cm.; sleeve width: 29 cm.
Mid- to latter half Edo period, latter half eighteenth to early nineteenth
century

Storybooks with various chapters from *The Tale of Genji* and characters
from poems on the subject are scattered randomly in this design. The storybooks are dyed either in crimson or indigo in *kanoko shibori* and stitch-
resist *shibori*, and the outlines later defined by brush painting. The titles
of the books are embroidered in colored threads, and the scattered characters from poems are embroidered in gold. The storybook motifs immediately recall the content of the stories. These motifs appear often in the
kosode hiinakata books around the first half of the eighteenth century,
when classic literature was particularly popular. It is apparent from the
even distribution of the motifs, the shapes of the *kanoko* dots, and the
embroidery techniques, that this *kosode* probably was made after the mid-
eighteenth century. A refined sense of design and a noble taste in literature
are portrayed harmoniously in this work.

The Tale of Genji is a novel written by Murasaki Shikibu in the mid-
Heian period (early eleventh century) and is a masterpiece of Japanese
literature. The story evolves around Hikaru Genji's successive love affairs
in and around the emperor's court in the early and mid-Heian period.
The story was a favorite theme for paintings and other decorative arts
from the Middle Ages to the Premodern Age. During the Edo period, as
publishing flourished, copies of *The Tale of Genji* reached enthusiastic
readers among the general public. The popularity of *The Tale of Genji*,
along with another representative story of the Heian period, *The Tale of
Ise*, as a literary motif in *kosode* decoration resulted from this broadened
audience.

25

26   *Kosode* with Scattered Plum Blossoms and Storybooks

Dye, embroidery, and *surihitta*
Light blue *chirimen* (crepe)
Height: 156 cm.; *yuki*: 60 cm.; sleeve length: 40 cm.; sleeve width: 30 cm.
Mid-Edo period, mid-eighteenth century

After the storybook and plum blossom motifs were reserved in white in a
scattered fashion over the *chirimen* (crepe) ground, the storybooks were
embroidered in "hidden" crimson stitches, and the pictures on the covers
of the books were embroidered in gold and colored threads. Pines, bamboo, plum trees, bush clover, cherry trees, young pines, Japanese larches,
bellflowers, clematis, cranes, weeping cherry trees, and chrysanthemums
are depicted on the covers of the books. Some plum blossom motifs are
executed in *surihitta* with *airō* (wax indigo) or *benigara* (Indian red). Others have only painted outlines or embroidered outlines in crimson or gold.
Still others have embroidered stamens. The original shoulder top was
located seven centimeters below the present shoulder top, which indicates
that this *kosode* was remade substantially in later years. The material of
the lining of this *kosode* is white *rinzu* (figured satin) with paulownias-
and-a-Chinese-phoenix diaper pattern, which is considered to have been
once a *kosode* itself. The lining is a later addition.

26

27   *Katabira* with Wisteria and Boats

Shibori, embroidery, and dye
White hemp
Height: 152 cm.; *yuki*: 57 cm.; sleeve length: 41 cm.; sleeve width: 28.5 cm.
Mid-Edo period, mid-eighteenth century

Wisteria and boat motifs are boldly displayed on the white hemp in this *katabira* (summer *kosode*). The shapes of the boat motifs are common to those of No. 19 and are seen often in *kosode* fashion books as formalized motifs. At a glance, the *kanoko* dots seem to have been created by *surihitta* stenciling but they must have been done by authentic *shibori* as there are many torn spots from sewing for the reserved areas in the *kanoko shibori* designs on the indigo blue ground. The light gray *kanoko*, on the other hand, is by *surihitta*.

The indigo blue boats and wisteria leaves are dyed by immersion dyeing (*tsukezome*) in indigo blue vats after the surrounding areas of the motifs are resisted in *shibori*.

The outlines of the boats, wisteria blossoms, leaves, and vines are embroidered in gold *koma* stitch and colored hidden stitch, *matoi* (twining) stitch, and *kakie* stitch with crimson and purple threads. The composition of large motifs boldly recalls the Kanbun style, but the dazzling wisteria, which fill the space as if the author was afraid to leave any open areas, show the spirit of the time after the Genroku culture matured.

27

28   *Katabira* with *Jarō* Basket, Cherry Blossoms, and Characters

Shibori, embroidery, and dye
Black hemp
Height: 141 cm., *yuki*: 60 cm., sleeve length: 44.5 cm., sleeve width: 31 cm.
Mid-Edo period, first half eighteenth century

Around the major motifs of the large *jarō* baskets, wave crests, cherry blossoms, and characters are arranged. A *jarō* is a round woven basket in which cobblestones and rubble are packed. These baskets were placed on the banks of rivers as a protective bulkhead and to control the water height. *Jarō* motifs are used often in summer *katabira* because they evoke images of cool, flowing water.

The process used to create this design is complex. After the *jarō* baskets and cherry blossoms have been resisted in capped *shibori* and the wave crests in *kanoko shibori*, the ground is dyed black in ink. The white reserved motifs are then outlined with brush painting. The woven patterns inside the baskets are expressed in a *kikkō* (tortoise-shell) pattern, *surihaku* (applied metallic leaf) with *airō* (wax indigo), and *bengara* (Indian red). Finally embroidery in gold and colored thread is added to the outlines of the *jarō* baskets and cherry blossoms, and characters are executed in gold thread *koma* stitch.

The characters are, from the right: *hō* (good), *ya* (field), *ka* (river), *ha* (waves), *ka* (flowers) on the back; and *ka* (smell), *gan* (wish), *ken* (to see), *hō* (mountain top), *shun* (spring) on the front. The technique of distributing the motifs around the waist is thought to date from the period after the Genroku style, or during the early half of the eighteenth century.

28

29   *Katabira* with Bundles of Maple and Cherry Branches

Shibori, embroidery, and dye
Black hemp
Height: 161 cm.; *yuki*: 60 cm.; sleeve length: 44 cm.; sleeve width: 31 cm.
Mid-Edo period, early half eighteenth century

The principle motif of bundles of maple and cherry branches, along with loose branches, is neatly arranged to cover the *kosode*. The technical process by which this is done is similar to that of the "*Katabira* with *Jarō* Baskets, Cherry Blossoms, and Characters" (No. 28). After the branches, blossoms, and areas surrounding the leaves have been resisted in stitch *shibori* or capped *shibori*, the ground is dyed black in ink. Then *surihitta* with *airō* (indigo wax) and *benigara* (Indian red) is applied to the maple leaves and cherry blossoms. Finally gold *koma* stitch is embroidered on the cords that tie the bundles and to the leaves. A characteristic of the Genroku style is present in the undecorated space around the waist area at left. As in No. 28, this *kosode* was probably made around the mid-Edo period, the early half of the eighteenth century.

29

30   *Katabira* with Plums and *Tsukiage* Doors

Shibori and embroidery
Black hemp
Height: 160 cm., *yuki*: 58 cm., sleeve length: 42 cm., sleeve width: 58 cm.
Mid-Edo period, mid-eighteenth century

Delicate plum trees rise from the skirt and two big *tsukiage* doors appear from the back to the right sleeve; another door appears on the skirt and yet another is visible on the lower left front of this *katabira* (summer *kosode*). A *tsukiage* door is a door whose upper edge is affixed to the lintel with fasteners such as hinges. Also called *aghe hisashi*, it is thrown open from inside with a stick. The *tsukiage* doors often appear as *kosode* motifs and some examples are recorded in *kosode* fashion books. For example, "A Design with *Tsukiaghe Door* and Wisteria-Arch Motifs" is recorded in *Sode Hiinakata*, published in 1612, while "A Design of *Tsukiage* Doors and Morning Glories" is recorded in *Tanzen Hiinakata*, published in 1704 (the first year of Hoei). In these designs the sticks used to throw open the doors are also drawn. This *kosode* shows no sticks, perhaps because by this time the *tsukiage* doors were formalized and established as motifs.

The bamboo weaving of the *tsukiage* doors is created by *kanoko shibori*. The plum blossoms on the doors are reserved white in capped *shibori* resist and are embroidered in gold and crimson; they are decorated by indigo blue and crimson *kanoko shibori*. The trunks are embroidered basically all in yellow-green satin stiches. It is interesting that even the bumps, holes, and moss of the trunk are realistically rendered by *norikake* and *matoi* (twining) embroidery techniques. The contrasting positioning of the motif on the lower left front and the motif on the skirt as well as the composition of the space are faithful to the Genroku style tradition. The emphasis on the right shoulder, with the left side remaining empty, shows the influence of the fading Kanbun style. But the ordered composition of the plum trees and the formalized expression do not at all suggest the bolder creativity of the early Edo period. This work probably dates from the mid-eighteenth century, after the Genroku period was over.

31   Screen with Two *Kosode*

Left:
Kosode fragment with chrysanthemums and bamboo (*magaki*) fence
Embroidery and *shibori*
White *rinzu* (figured satin)
Mid-Edo period, late seventeenth to early eighteenth century

The chrysanthemums and *magaki* (rough, woven bamboo fence) are rendered in *shibori* dyeing and embroidery. The central motifs, the thunderbolt shapes of the *magaki* and the round chrysanthemums, are depicted in crimson and indigo blue *kanoko shibori*. The indigo *kanoko* dots are a little uneven in their size, but the crimson *kanoko* dots are evenly sized and distributed. The *kanoko* dots seem to be a form which marked the transition between the Kanbun and Genroku styles. The small clusters of chrysanthemum flowers and the leaves are embroidered, as is the *magaki* fence in gold *koma* stitch. The blue-gray embroidery seems to be a later addition. During the Heian period, chrysanthemums were usually planted against *magaki* fences; the combination was a frequent sight in gardens. Later, in the Kamakura period, depictions of actual scenes of everyday life were fashionable, and this motif was used in *makie* (lacquer). This *kosode* makes use of the traditional combination of chrysanthemums and bamboo (*magaki*) fence as its central motif. In the skirt area, pines and bamboo grass are embroidered. All these motifs suggest an auspicious intent of this design. The expression of the chrysanthemums in *kanoko shibori* and the combination of the *shibori* and embroidery techniques resemble those of the *kosode* with chrysanthemum shrubs in No. 13. This *kosode* must date from the same period, from the late seventeenth to the early eighteenth century.

Kosode fragment with morning glories
Shibori, dyeing, and embroidery
Crimson *chirimen* (crepe)
Late Edo period, nineteenth century

Morning glories blooming in profusion and covering the bamboo fence
are beautifully designed on a bright crimson background. The applied
techniques are *shibori* dyeing, paste-resist dyeing, and painting in indigo-
type pigments. The process of the dyeing is not entirely clear. First the
ground was dyed in saffron yellow, with the morning glory blossoms in
capped *shibori* resist. When the ground was dyed crimson, it was not
uncommon to dye the ground first in saffron yellow in order to achieve a
better crimson color. But the next step in the process is not clear. How
were the leaves and stems resisted, and how was the ground dyed in crimson? Could it have been paste dyed? Normally vat dyeing is applied to dye
the whole ground in crimson, just like the vat dyeing in indigo blue; the
paste must be applied from both the front and back surfaces of the material. If the resist paste is applied only to one side of the material, the depth
of color differs from one side to the other.

A remnant of the *kosode*, left over after the other fragments were mounted
on the screen, is still preserved in the Nomura Collection. Study of this
remnant shows that, although the paste was applied only from one side,
there is very little difference in the shades of the colors on both sides of
the material. Maybe the paste was applied to only the motifs on the front
surface. It is necessary to repeat the dipping process many times in vat
dyeing of both indigo dye and crimson dye. It can be deduced that the
repeated dipping made the dye penetrate to the back so that the difference
in shades was unnoticeable. It also can be reasonably deduced that a little
blurring in the outlines of the motifs was caused by the melting of the
resist paste around the motif areas. All these deductions are still based on
speculation, and more study is needed. There is another hypothesis that
after the background had been dyed in crimson, the crimson color on the
motifs was discharged to expose the yellow by means of the discharge
dyeing (*nukizome*) technique. It is impossible, however, to discharge a natural dye so completely. Only modern synthetic dyes can be so discharged.
Thus that speculation appears implausible. Another fragment thought to
have belonged to the same *kosode* exists in the Tōyama Memorial Museum
in Kawagoe City in Saitama prefecture.

32   Screen with Two *Kosode*

Left:
Kosode fragment with curtains, weeping cherry trees, and drying fishnet
Yūzen dyeing and embroidery
White *chirimen* (crepe)
Mid-Edo period, late eighteenth century

On the background of white-reserved curtains and indigo-dyed water, the drooping branches of the double flowered cherry trees leisurely sway. A fishnet pattern and various shells are depicted on the skirt. *Yūzen* dyeing and additional embroidery are used to render this design. The lively composition and the clever continuity of the curtains, wave crests, and fishnet hint at the author's good sense of design. A fishnet hung to dry over a stake on the beach is incorporated into the pattern. Drying fishnet patterns often appear as *kosode* motifs, especially among *kosode* of the Kanbun style, after the mid-seventeenth century. Usually they are not presented as mere fishnets but are incorporated, in many cases, into elaborate designs. For example, some fishnets are disguised as bamboo shoots. To the drying fishnet pattern of this *kosode* other decorations, such as a *kumo-maru* (clouds in a circle) pattern, chrysanthemums, peonies, and a *shippō-tsunagi* (combined seven treasures) pattern are added.

As was explained in an earlier essay, in the usual *yūzen* process, the outlines of the motifs were paste resisted and then the various pigments were brush painted. Afterward, the motifs themselves were resisted in paste and the whole background dyed in *hikizome* (brush dyeing). The indigo dyeing is an exception. The ground is immersion dyed, especially when a large area such as this one is dyed. In this fragment no fine lines of the paste characteristic to *yūzen* dyeing are visible in the border lines between the indigo blue motifs and motifs in other colors. This is because the *yūzen* dyeing was done after the indigo dyeing by immersion. The witty design and flashy coloring are characteristic of *yūzen* dyeing, and thus this *kosode* probably dates during the peak period of *yūzen* dyeing, the mid-Edo period.

Right:
Kosode fragment in divided-background style with maples beside water
Yūzen dyeing, embroidery, and *surihitta*
Chirimen (crepe)
Mid-Edo period, mid-eighteenth century

On the skirt, mandarin ducks can be seen floating on the water. The surrounding areas are reserved white in wave-crest shapes, over which is depicted an inlet of a swamp where grass and chrysanthemums grow. On the upper half, maple trees spread their branches lightly. All of these motifs are executed by *yūzen* dyeing along with gold and colored embroidery and *surihitta*. The painting (*irosashi*) of *yūzen* dyeing is done either with a big paintbrush or with a brush for drawings. The peculiarity of the motifs of this *kosode* is found in the ample use of *bokashi* (gradation technique), in which another color is added to the motif before the first color dye dries. This design makes a very flamboyant impression. There are signs of carelessness in some details, such as the blurred dye coming out of the fine lines of the paste and rough ink lines defining the maple leaves. This work probably dates from the later years of the mid-Edo period, when *yūzen* dyeing was firmly established.

33   Screen with Two *Kosode*

Left:
Kosode fragment in divided-background style with flowing water, maples,
and autumn grass
Yūzen dyeing
Chirimen (crepe)
Mid-Edo period, latter half eighteenth century

The background is dyed in *somewake* into cloud shapes in crimson
shibori. Between these cloud shapes, a stream on which maple leaves float
and bank areas with groups of pinks and bellflowers are depicted by *yūzen*
dyeing. The blurs visible in the surrounding areas of the crimson-dyed
parts were caused during the *shibori* dyeing process. The *hikizome* (brush
dyeing of the whole ground), which is characteristic to *yūzen* dyeing, is
not suited to dyeing in crimson, nor can one adapt the immersion dyeing
with paste resist of the indigo. The only dependable technique for dying in
crimson was *shibori*. Another reason for the abundant use of *shibori*
dyeing in crimson, which cannot be ignored, is the special love the Japanese had toward the blurs and gradations characteristic of *shibori* dyeing.
The present composition may have been altered from the original, which
seems to have been in dan (alternating bands) with cloud shapes as its
central motifs. This represents a type of *yūzen* dyeing of the mid-
eighteenth century.

Right:
Kosode fragment in divided-background style with autumn flowers and plovers
Yūzen dyeing
Saya (figured twill)
Mid-Edo period, eighteenth century

Over the background, scattered with triangles, autumn flowers such as chrysanthemums, bellflowers, lilies, and bush clover are placed. This composition, with triangles as its central design, is called *minato dori* (harbor composition). The purple triangles are executed in *shibori*, and inside these shapes flying plovers are reserved white in capped *shibori* and *kanoko shibori*. Other motifs are executed in *yūzen* dyeing. The slightly blurred light blue seen around the motifs dyed in indigo seems to have been caused by immersion dyeing.

The simplified chrysanthemums and bellflowers are a "Kōrin design." Ogata Kōrin (1658–1716) was one of the master painters of the mid-Edo period. He admired the decorative painting styles of Kōetsu and Sōtatsu and developed his own bold, flamboyant style. As was stated in an earlier essay on the Kanbun style, Kōrin was born in the household of the dry goods dealer Kariganeya and so was acquainted with the various designs of dyed goods and weavings. In addition to his paintings, he produced many excellent craft works. One example is a *kakie* (brush painted) *kosode*, "*Kosode* with Winter Trees," which is preserved in the Tokyo National Museum. Probably because of the influence of this "*Kosode* with Winter Trees," Kōrin's designs became very popular.

The popularity of Kōrin's designs can be linked to the fashion book *Tō-fū Bijo Hiinakata* (*Today's Beauties' Fashion Book*), published in 1715. This book was the first to list designs inspired by Kōrin. After its publication, fashion books with subtitles of *Tosei Kōrin* (*The Contemporary Kōrin*) and *Kōrin Moyō* (*Kōrin Designs*) were published successively until the mid-eighteenth century.

On the back of this screen a fragment of a lining containing ink writing is attached, which reads: "Donated by Kimura Gihei, for I Tei-en, the chief priest of the Yōrenji temple, Kokyo Kurita district, Yakura village, who died at four o'clock in the afternoon, February 29, 1740." That the inscribed fragment was taken from the lining of the *kosode* attached to the screen cannot be proven. If it were so—and it is plausible in that the 1740 date corresponds to the period when Kōrin designs are thought to have been in fashion—it would be a very important source of proof that Kōrin designs were in fact popular then.

34   *Kosode* in Divided-Background with Views of the Eastern
Part of the City of Kyoto

Yūzen dyeing and embroidery
Chirimen (crepe)
Height: 153 cm.; *yuki*: 62 cm.; sleeve length: 45 cm.; sleeve width: 27.5 cm.
Mid-Edo period, mid-eighteenth century

Scenic locations in the eastern part of Kyoto are depicted in a composition recalling *rakuchu-rakugai-zu* (screen design of sights in and around Kyoto). The large structure depicted on the upper back is the Kiyomizu Temple. This is contiguous to the Otowa Falls on the right sleeve. Directly below Kiyomizu Temple, Yasaka-Pagoda stands tall. A view of Gojō Bridge over the Kamo River spreads across the skirt. Scenery motifs like this one are well suited to *yūzen* dyeing, used for its pictorial potential. Many examples of *yūzen* works with scenic motifs have been found, including those in such fashion books as "Designs of Mountains and Water Flow" in *Nishikawa Hinigata*, published in 1718; "Ōmi Hakkei" ("Eight Scenic Places in Ōmi") in *Ehon Hinagata Fudan Sakura*, published in 1720; "Tō Hakkei" in *Kōrin Hinakata Wakamitori*, published in May 1727; *Shosiki Hinagata Hanamiguruma*, published from 1704 until 1710; *Hinagata Tatsutagawa*, published in July 1742; and many others. It is known from these examples that *yūzen* designs with scenic views were popular from the first half to the mid-eighteenth century.

It is customary to embroider *yūzen*-dyed works so as to add a stereoscopic effect which surpasses the flat presentation resulting from dyeing alone. On the golden cloud shapes, which have been dyed in *somewake* in saffron yellow, plum tree and cherry tree branches are embroidered in colored and gold threads to produce a colorful impression. The golden cloud shapes are very effective both as a decorative device and in making the vast distances and relationships between places believable. Usually in *yūzen somewake* (divided background) *shibori* dyeing is used. Normally the blurred outlines of the *shibori* are not corrected in order to preserve the impression of *shibori*, as can be seen in the examples in *yūzen* fashion books. In this *kosode* the clarity of the outlines of the golden clouds are suggestive of *yūzen* dyeing; however, needle holes from *shibori* remain around the outlines of the gold clouds. It is doubtful that the outlines were delineated after the shapes had been dyed in *shibori*. This remains a

mystery. The overlapping hems and parts of the neckbands are later additions. The sleeves have been shortened and are thought to have been *furisode* originally.

| 35 | *Kosode* with Wisteria and *Shōji* Doors |

Yūzen dyeing and embroidery
Antwerp blue *chirimen* (crepe)
Height: 145 cm.; *yuki*: 60 cm.; sleeve length: 43 cm.; sleeve width: 32 cm.
Mid-Edo period, mid-eighteenth century

Wisteria blossoms hang from the shoulders to both sleeves. *Shōji* door motifs appear in a bold diagonal from the side sleeve to the skirt, on which pine needles are scattered. The indigo background symbolizes an evening scene, and the brightness of the *shōji* doors represent the lights from inside the house. The wisteria arch and the scattered pine needles in the dark evening garden are silhouetted dimly by the light reflected from inside. *Yūzen* dyeing and embroidery techniques are equally used. In *yūzen* of the Edo period the ground was not always dyed by brush (*hikizome*). The background of this *kosode* was dyed by dipping in a vat of indigo blue. In this process every motif to be dyed in indigo was paste resisted. The resist paste was applied also from the reverse side of the material for the larger motifs such as the *shōji* doors. The process of immersion dyeing must have been repeated several times to attain this dark shade of indigo. While indigo blue can be made into a pigment for *hikizome* (brush) dyeing, the technique is not easily applied to a large area; in order to achieve a deeper color, only the traditional immersion dyeing can be used.

After the background was dyed in indigo blue, a thin line of paste was applied on portions of the white reserved *shōji* doors and wisteria leaves and then they were brush painted, all of which are aspects of the *yūzen* process. The pine needles and wisteria blossoms are reserved in white, and, by marking the dots from the reverse side with a stick, the artist added *kanoko*-like effects to the wisteria blossoms. The entire process was completed by embroidery in color and gold. The color of the threads and the techniques used indicate that the embroidery on the blue-gray areas is new; probably the original embroidery was lost. The shoulder line is off by 18 centimeters toward the front, and the right sleeve line is off by 6.5 centimeters toward the front also. If the corrections were made, the designs of the front and the back would be continuous at both sides. The original composition is known to have been more three-dimensional and natural-looking. The altered position of the right sleeve line proves that the original sleeve length was at least 50 centimeters, which indicates that this was a *furisode*.

Incorporating the parts of a building, such as *shōji* doors, into a kimono design may seem peculiar, but the Japanese like *shōji* motifs and they frequently appear in *kosode*. Another example of *kosode* with *shōji* motifs is in the Keichō style and dates from the early Edo period. Several others are illustrated in *kosode* fashion books of the mid-Edo period, like the fashion book published in 1704, but none shows the *shōji* design as such an up-to-date and bold fashion as this *kosode* does. Interestingly, almost the same design is recorded in the *kosode* fashion book *Kōrin Hiinakata Wakamitori*, published in 1727. It is included in an instructional section titled "The Evening Wisteria":

> Ground in deep blue or black or brown; wisteria in white reserve with occasional *kanoko*; *shōji* in white, frames in narrow dye (*hosozome*); wisteria poked from the back; ink paint the pine needles on the lower skirt. Dark brown pine needles in white reserve can be thin.

The process used in creating this *kosode* corresponds almost exactly to that given above. The design is characteristic of the style of the Genroku period (1688–1704), although this *kosode* must have been made not much later than 1727, the year the first edition of *Kōrin Hiinakata Wakamitori* was published.

36   *Furisode* with Wisteria, Stream, and Irises

Yūzen dyeing and embroidery
.Light blue *chirimen* (crepe)
Height: 148 cm.; *yuki*: 59 cm.; sleeve length: 90.5 cm.; sleeve width: 30 cm.
Mid-Edo period, mid-eighteenth century

Wisteria blossoms spill over the woven bamboo arch from the waistline to the sleeves, while the water flows around the irises on the skirts from the waistline down. The design above the waistline is in bilateral symmetry, but the design below the waistline rises diagonally from the left skirt to the right side, where irises and water motifs are scattered at the bottom of the right sleeve. The Genroku tradition is evident in the empty left side and the design on the lower left front to the design on the back skirt. The definite separation of the design between the lower and upper portions of the kimono suggests a mid-eighteenth-century date. The primary technique applied was *yūzen* dyeing; some gold and color embroidery was added. The outlines of some irises and wisteria leaves were painted in crimson. The light blue color of the ground apparently was dyed by immersion, but since the the color is light, the ground was immersed in dye only twice at most. It should have been sufficient just to apply the resist paste to the surface of the material. The discountinuity of the design of the front skirt is caused by the fact that approximately six centimeters of the front is sewn into the overlap (*okumi*); it is guessed that this *kosode* was remade in later years.

In May and June, long clusters of lavender or white butterfly-shaped blossoms color wisteria. Irises grow in ponds or swamps and produce large six-petaled blossoms in early summer. An iris blossom is usually purple or white, three of its six petals resembling a sparrow with its wings open. These irises are called *kakitsubata*, a name derived from the Chinese characters meaning "sparrow-flowers." The design from *kosode* fashion books entitled "A Design of Seeing the Sparrows as Irises" shows an image of flying sparrows which also represent iris blossoms. Both wisteria and irises are representative of Japanese summer vegetation and appear frequently in *kosode* design.

36

37   *Furisode* with Curtains (*Manmaku*), Cherries, and Maples

Yūzen dyeing
Antwerp blue *chirimen* (crepe)
Height: 163 cm.; *yuki*: 60 cm.; sleeve length: 90 cm.; sleeve width: 31 cm.
Mid-Edo period, mid-eighteenth century

Motifs combining *manmaku* curtains with cherry and maple trees, which
represent each spring and autumn season, are distributed in rhythmic
movement all over this *kosode*. *Manmaku* is a decorative curtain made of
a patchwork material. It is one of the popular motifs in *kosode* design;
No. 68 is an example.

With this *kosode*, the motifs were paste resisted and dipped in a vat of
indigo blue, reserving the curtains and trees in white. It seems that, at this
stage, the resist paste was applied from both sides of the material. This is
evidenced by the fact that the indigo blue color of the ground is deep, and
to attain this deepness the process of the vat dyeing must have been
repeated several times. Then the insides of the curtains were decorated.
The technique used was identical to today's *yūzen* dyeing technique in
which the outlines of the motifs are resisted with fine lines of paste and
the motifs decorated with colorful brush painting. However, today's *yūzen*
involves painting the motif details first. After the paint dries, motifs are
reserved in paste resist and then the ground is dyed in *hikizome* (brush
painting over the whole material). In other words, the dyeing of the
ground is left until the final stage. This became possible after many kinds
of synthetic dye were made available for *hikizome*. At least until the mid-
Edo period, the dyeing of the ground had always been done by immersion.
Today *yūzen* dyeing by immersion technically is not practiced at all.
Another method of dyeing by immersion after the *yūzen* painting has been
completed has been forgotten. Theoretically, it is possible to complete the
details first, then provide the paste resist, and finally dye the ground by
immersion. However, in the premodern *yūzen* the first step usually taken
was the immersion dyeing of the ground. This conclusion is supported in
Yūzen Hiinakata, published in 1688:

> 1. In *yūzen* dyeing, a sketch of each favorite motif should be
>   drawn first. Then apply the paste or tie it up for dyeing. Dye
>   the ground into divided sections (*somewake*). After dyeing

the ground, do not touch up the surounding areas of *shibori* lines by brush painting, but paint the sketches for the decoration in the motifs.

2. Dye each motif with the sketch in separate colors (*somewake*) then provide *nuihaku* (embroidery and metallic leaf) *kanoko shibori* and brush painting in the motifs.

As is stated clearly above, the dyeing of the ground was done prior to the painting in the motifs.

There is a definite difference between the areas painted with fine lines of paste and the areas dyed by immersion. While the decorations in the *manmaku* curtains, outlined with the white fine lines of the paste, are clear and vivid, the outlines of the curtain separating the motifs from the indigo blue background and the outlines of the cherry and maple trees are blurred. This design successfully illustrates the contrast between the two dyeing techniques, which results in a three-dimensional effect.

38   *Kosode* with Bush Clover and Woven Bamboo Fences

Yūzen dyeing and embroidery
Azure *chirimen* (crepe)
Height: 156 cm.; *yuki*: 62.5 cm.; sleeve length: 44 cm.; sleeve width: 30.5 cm.
Mid- to late Edo period, late eighteenth century

In this motif the bush clover is combined with various fence forms and scattered all over the *kosode*. None of the telltale white outlines of *yūzen* dyeing remain in the bush clover motifs, indicating that the ground was dyed first with the motifs in paste resist, and the motifs painted after the

paste washed away, as was done in No. 37. The leaves are outlined with fine resist-paste lines and painted in yellow; they are haloed with an indigo-blue-type pigment. The blossoms are embroidered in white *matoi* (twinning) stitch. The fences and the leaves are touched with gold and color embroidery.

A design akin to this *kosode* is recorded in the *kosode* fashion book *Hiinagata Itoyanaghi*, published in 1776. Except for screens which take the place of fences, the designs of "Screens and Bush Clovers" in this fashion book correspond almost exactly to those of this *kosode*. The record in this fashion book is not an atypical case. This type of scattered-motif design was popular during the late eighteenth century. This *kosode* probably was created during or after the eighteenth century.

39   *Kosode* with Water and Wildflowers

Paste dyeing and embroidery
Kurobeni (dark brown) *rinzu* (figured satin)
Height: 156.5 cm.; *yuki*: 62.5 cm.; sleeve length: 40.5 cm.;
sleeve width: 33 cm.
Mid-Edo period, mid-eighteenth century

A Kōrin-style wavy stream, surrounded by wildflowers similar to the firefly-cage lilies, rolls from the left skirt to the right sleeve on the back. The same design is repeated symmetrically on the front. The technique used here is based on paste dyeing, which differs from *yūzen* dyeing. The design was achieved as follows: first, the ground was dyed in azure after resiste paste was applied to the areas that appear white and yellow. After the paste was washed away, each motif, that is, the outline of every wave, flower, and blade of grass, was resisted in fine lines with paste and dyed in *kurobeni* (dark brown). The paste was washed away a second time, and

the flowers were reserved in white and the stems in blue. Yellow was added to parts of the flowers and stems. Finally the outlines of the blossoms were defined by ink painting. One can conclude that the process of *irosashi* (added brush painting) in *yūzen* dyeing was included in the ground dyeing process of this *kosode*. The Nomura Collection includes another *kosode* of very similar design; perhaps the buyer ordered several *kosode* of the same design for reasons unknown.

40   *Kosode* with Chrysanthemums in Alternating Bands

Yūzen dyeing and *shibori*
Saffron yellow *rinzu* (figured satin)
Height: 155 cm.; *yuki*: 61.5 cm.; sleeve length: 42 cm.; sleeve width: 32 cm.
Late Edo period, early nineteenth century

A series of chrysanthemums are placed horizontally in four bands in "arranged *dangawari*" (alternating bands). Purple blossoms appear on the upper band, white on the second band, and red on the lower two bands. Variety is also achieved by dyeing the leaves in blue on the second band and green on the other three bands in *yūzen* dyeing. The design is organized in a bilateral symmetry, with the horizontal effects characteristic of the late Edo period. The process probably was executed as follows: first the ground was immersion dyed in saffron yellow, with the motifs in paste resist. After the paste was washed away, fine resist-paste lines were applied to the outlines of the stems, leaves, and veins. Then they were brush painted. Finally the blossoms, reserved in white, were dyed by *shibori* after the surrounding areas were tied for resist. In the Nomura Collection there is a dark brown *kosode* fragment with chrysanthemum motifs in *dangawari* design that was created in the same manner, which is evidence that this kind of design was often reproduced.

40

41 *Furisode* in Divided-Background Style with
Flower-Covered Rafts

Yūzen dyeing, embroidery, and dyeing
Chirimen (crepe)
Height: 152 cm.; *yuki*: 62 cm.; sleeve length: 94.5 cm.; sleeve
width: 32 cm.
Later half Edo period, first half nineteenth century

Rafts and fallen cherry blossoms float on the water from the lower halves
of the sleeves to the areas below the waist on the body of this *furisode*, as
if it were a picture drawn on a canvas. In the upper purple area cherry
branches are arranged artistically. The cherry blossoms have been paste
resisted; the upper half of the ground is *shibori*-dyed in purple and the
skirt is dyed in grey *usuzumi* (thin Indian ink). The shading technique
used around the waist is called dyeing. After the ground has been dyed
rafts and leaves are executed by *yūzen* dyeing. Then the stamens of the
cherry blossoms are painted in pigments. Gold couching is added to decorate parts of the leaves and the ropes that tie the rafts. The fallen cherry
blossoms on the rafts are embroidered. The composition exhibits the
bilateral symmetry of the late Edo style, which can be considered a developed form of *Edozuma* design. The same design appears on the lining of
the skirt. Other designs for *kosode* linings are found in *Tosei-moyō
Hiinakata Chitosegusa*, which was published in 1754, and *Hiinakata
Sodenoyama*, published in 1757. The lining design gradually increased in
popularity until the nineteenth century. The design of this *furisode* is
thought to have been created during the first half of the nineteenth century, after the standard designs of the late Edo style had been established.

41

142

42 *Furisode* with Butterflies in Clouds and Bush Clover

Yūzen dyeing and *shibori*
Gray *chirimen* (crepe)
Height: 140 cm.; *yuki*: 55 cm.; sleeve length: 80 cm.; sleeve width: 55 cm.
Latter half Edo period, nineteenth century

Cloud-shaped motifs with fluttering butterflies and bush clover with lovely white blossoms are arranged in bilateral symmetry in this *furisode*, with empty space left around the waist. The purple clouds are executed in *shibori* dyeing; some of the hemp threads from the *shibori* process remain untied. Other motifs are executed in *yūzen* dyeing. Outlines of the bush clover blossoms and butterflies are touched-up with ink painting. The yellow-ocher, blue, purple, and green on the gray background create a subdued impression, even though the long sleeves indicate that it is a young woman's *furisode*. It must reflect the taste of the latter half of the Edo period.

During the latter half of the Edo period standardized designs again came into fashion in reaction to the popular pictorial motifs of *yūzen* dyeing. But the standard designs of this period differed from those of the Genroku style in their basic bilateral symmetry and in the small size of the motifs. Another characteristic of the standard designs of this period is the continuation of the motifs around the skirt from the right overlap to the left overlap. The remaking of this *furisode* seems to have followed the original faithfully. It is peculiar that the lower edges of neckbands to lower edges of overlaps are short.

42

43   *Furisode* in Divided-Background Style with Plovers,
Pine Trees on the Seashore, Seaweed, and Shells

Yūzen dyeing, brush painting, and embroidery
Aya (figured twill)
Height: 150 cm.; *yuki*: 61 cm.; sleeve length: 97 cm.; sleeve width: 31 cm.
Late Edo period, early to mid-nineteenth century

The peony and vine scroll (*karakusa*) pattern of the fabric is woven with
three weft *aya* silk. It is dyed in *somewake* (divided background) in three
bands of azure, white, and ocher. The upper band is decorated with plo-
ver motifs, the middle band with sailboats and seashore pines, and the
lower band with shells and seaweed. The three bands symbolize, from top
to bottom, the sky, the ocean, and the land. The designer plays with the
symbolism by transforming the ocean into clouds at the upper edge of the
middle band; the land suddenly is transformed into the inside of the
ocean where the designer dyed seaweed in the lower skirt. The smallness
of each motif and the clear bilateral symmetry are common characteristics
of *kosode* of the late Edo period. Paste-resist dyeing and *yūzen* dyeing are
the primary techniques used, with ink painting added to the plovers and
shells at the end of the process; embroidery is added to portions of the
sails.

43

44   *Furisode* with Stream and Chrysanthemums

Yūzen dyeing
Light blue *rinzu* (figured satin)
Height: 150 cm.; *yuki*: 62 cm.; sleeve length: 95 cm.; sleeve width: 30 cm.
Latter half Edo period, first half to mid-nineteenth century

A stream and the chrysanthemums growing thickly on its banks are depicted by *yūzen* dyeing in this *furisode*; apparent is the same bilaterally symmetrical composition of the *furisode* in No. 43. Among the standard-ized designs in bilateral symmetry of the latter half of the Edo period are those in which the motifs spread along the lower edges of the neckbands to the skirt. These are *Edozuma* designs, which are known to have been popular between the latter half of the eighteenth and the early half of the nineteenth century, judging from the publishing dates of the fashion books that included similar designs. The most characteristic feature of *Edozuma* is that very small motifs are repeated and scattered or lined up. Composi-tions in which the motifs are united to express one continuous design are seldom seen. *Edozuma* designs in *kosode* fashion books usually have no decorations on the shoulders or around the chest. The design of this *kosode* is an exception. *Kikusui*, which combines chrysanthemums and flowing water, is one of the auspicious motifs. The diaper pattern on the *rinzu* is also auspicious, with the *shippō-tsunagi* (seven-treasures) motif and the plums, bamboo, and young-pines-in-the-circle motifs. Because of the combination of these felicitous motifs this may be a wedding *furisode*. The discontinuity of the design between the sleeves and the body is caused by careless remaking, at which time the sleeves were attached to the wrong sides.

44

45   *Furisode* in Divided-Background Style with *Genji-kō*
    (Incense) and Trailing Plants

Yūzen dyeing

Chirimen (crepe)

Height: 150 cm.; *yuki*: 62 cm.; sleeve length: 99 cm.; sleeve width: 32 cm.

Latter half Edo period, first half to mid-nineteenth century

A very light blue *chirimen* background is dyed in *somewake* (divided background) into gray *suhama* (sandy-beach) motifs in a *furisode* with an *Edozuma* design that is positioned slightly higher on the robe than usual. *Genji-kō* and trailing plants are executed in *yūzen* dyeing in the grey areas. *Genji-kō* is one of several kinds of incense used in *kōdō* (a ceremonial game of burning and smelling incense). In this game five kinds of incense are divided and wrapped into five bags, for a total of twenty-five bags. From the twenty-five bags, five are chosen at random and burned. The competitor guesses whether the five bags contain the same kind or different kinds of incense. There are fifty-two possible combinations of incense to identify. In *genji-kō* motifs, the fifty-two combinations possible in the incense game are designed to correspond to all but two of the fifty-four stories of *The Tale of Genji*; the first story, "Kiritsubo," and the last, "Yume-no-ukihashi," have not been made into motifs. The motif of *genji-kō* of this *kosode* symbolizes the story "Tamakatsura," which is the name of the story's heroine, who was Tō Nō Chūjō's child by Yūgao and later was brought up by Genji. *Tamakatsura* is now a general term for trailing plants, represented in this *furisode*. It is a representative work of the later Edo period, characterized by sparse depictions and subdued coloring.

45

46   *Furisode* in Divided-Background Style with Beach Pines
      and Cranes

Yūzen dyeing
Chirimen (crepe)
Height: 152 cm.; *yuki*: 60 cm.; sleeve length: 10 cm.; sleeve width: 29 cm.
Later half Edo period, mid-nineteenth century

A bird's eye view of beach pines, flying cranes, and islands visible in the
distance are portrayed here. This *furisode* has the bilaterally symmetrical
composition characteristic of the standard design of the late Edo period.
The *somewake* (divided background) in light blue and ocher lends a
shibori effect to the garment when in fact no *shibori* dyeing was used. The
somewake is achieved by paste resist, and *bokashi* (shading) was added
later. The basic technique is *yūzen* dyeing. At the end, the islands are
painted in colors and the cranes are painted in ink. Gold-thread embroidery also has been added. The motifs are small in size and they lack
rhythmical movement. The scenery recedes as it stretches from the skirt to
the shoulders; the cresting waves depicted on the skirt are closest to the
viewer, and the islands on the shoulders appear distant. This composition
and the witty rendering of the wave crests reflect the virtuous taste of the
late Edo period.

46

47   *Kosode* with Pines and Sails

Shibori and embroidery
Navy blue *rinzu* (figured satin)
Height: 151.5 cm.; *yuki*: 62 cm.; sleeve length: 43 cm.; sleeve width: 32 cm.
Latter half Edo period, nineteenth century

Sailboat and wave-crest motifs are depicted from the skirt to the waist,
and mounds and pine trees are composed in a *chirashi* (scattered) design
above the waist in this elegant *kosode*. The mounds, pines, and sails are
executed in *kanoko shibori* and capped *shibori*, with additional embroidery in gold *koma* stitch and colored hidden stitch as well as painting.
The crest of the waves are embroidered in white *matsui* (twining) stitch.
The sensitivity of this seemingly simple design can be seen in the treat-
ment of some special details: the sailboats appear smaller as they sail
away from the viewer, indicating a proper sense of perspective on the part
of the designer; in addition, the *kanoko* dots in the mounds are smaller in
size than those of the sailboats, resulting in a three-dimensional effect.
Although this work lacks rhythmical movement and freshness, it gives a
sense of the secure and graceful atmosphere of the late Edo period.

47

48   Unlined *Furisode* with Pine, Plum, Bamboo Grass, Reed, Clouds, and Waterfall

Dye and embroidery
Purple silk gauze
Height: 167 cm.; *yuki*: 63.5 cm.; sleeve length: 97 cm.; sleeve width: 31.5 cm.
Late Edo period, end eighteenth century to first half nineteenth century

This is a typical upper military class *furisode*, a landscape with a waterfall gushing from the side of a mountain on which cherry trees, pines, and reeds densely grow. The waterfall is reserved white with paste resist, and embroidered in color and in gold. The presence of a bundle of brushwood and a gourd placed under the waterfall suggest that this is not an ordinary landscape design. Rather, it is a scene taken from *Yōrōnotaki*, a Nō play. *Yōrōnotaki* is the story of a woodcutter who is devoted to his parents. Because of his virtue a spiritual spring appears in Yōrōnotaki (literally, "the waterfall of caring for the aged") in the country of Mino. In the upper military class *kosode* of the late Edo period, the frequent adding of embroidery to areas reserved white by paste resist stereotyped their designs. In these uniform patterns, probably in order to show one's individuality, many attempts were made to adapt stories and morals from various literary sources to *kosode* designs. While they are never expressed directly, these morals and stories are alluded to in the form of riddles and clues, requiring the viewer to be able to understand the hidden meaning. This was possible only among the educated and cultured of the period. For this reason, there are quite a few extant examples of designs of this type, such as Nos. 50 and 51, whose meaning we no longer can comprehend.

48

49   Unlined *Furisode* with Autumn Grass Scenery with People, Plovers, and Streams

Dye and embroidery
Antwerp blue *nando* (silk gauze)
Height: 154.5 cm.; *yuki*: 59 cm.; sleeve length: 92 cm.; sleeve width: 30.5 cm.
Late Edo period, end of eighteenth century to first half nineteenth century

---

This is a typical *kosode* for the aristocracy of the late Edo period. The white reserved motifs stand out against the ground, which is dyed in Antwerp blue with paste resist. Color and gold embroidery, ink painting, and touch-up dyed figures are added to the motifs. Since this is a silk gauze *furisode*, it must have been worn by a young woman in summer. The scenery covers the whole surface of the *kosode*. The area from the waist to the skirt signifies the land, and the area from the waist to the shoulders depicts the sky, in which many plovers fly. At the center of the skirt a river, a person on horseback, and *yamabuki* flowers (Japanese roses) appear. The scene is based on an ancient poem which reads as follows:

Koma tome te	Let us stop the horse
iza mizu kawan	And give it water
yamabuki no	From Idenotamagawa,
hana no kage sou	Over which the yamabuki blossoms
ide no tamagawa.	Cast their shadows.

Idenotamagawa, located in Kyoto prefecture, was famous since ancient times for the *yamabuki* on its banks. The flying plovers probably allude to Nodanotamagawa, also called Chidorinotamagawa ("Plovers' River"), which flowed in Miyagi prefecture. Idenotamagawa and Nodanotamagawa had been famous places of *waka* poem reading. There were six loved rivers that were referred to as "Rokutamagawa" ("Six Rivers").

49

50   Unlined *Kosode* with Chrysanthemums, Haystacks, Rooster, and Chicken

Embroidery
Light green figured silk gauze
Height: 175 cm.; *yuki*: 62 cm.; sleeve length: 44 cm.; sleeve width: 31 cm.
Late Edo period, end eighteenth to early nineteenth century

The area from the waist to the skirt of this light green figured silk gauze *kosode* is filled with beautifully embroidered motifs of chrysanthemums, reeds, rice haystacks, and a *shiorido* (a door made of woven branches). A chicken is visible on the upper overlap of the garment, and a rooster struts across the back of the skirt; the birds are embroidered realistically. A *misu* (bamboo blind) is visible diagonally left and above the rooster, which may allude to a story whose source is not known. This probably was a summer garment worn in an upper military class household during the late Edo period.

50

51   *Kosode* with Waterfall, Blossoms, and Sparrows

Dye and embroidery
Light blue *chirimen* (crepe)
Height: 178 cm.; *yuki*: 64 cm.; sleeve length: 46 cm.; sleeve width: 33 cm.
Late Edo period, late eighteenth to first half nineteenth century

---

The three-leafed-mallow-in-the-circle crest of the Tokugawa shogunal family identifies this *kosode* with the military elite class of the late Edo period. The embroidered motifs, reserved in white, are concentrated on the areas under the waistline. In this mountain scene, cherry trees, wisteria, pines, and reeds are dense and interlocking. Sparrows soar gracefully over a waterfall that cascades over a cliff. The depiction of the deep mountain scene is not one of loneliness but of solemnity, in its beautiful adornment of the cherry and wisteria blossoms. Most likely, the garment was part of a great warrior's wardrobe.

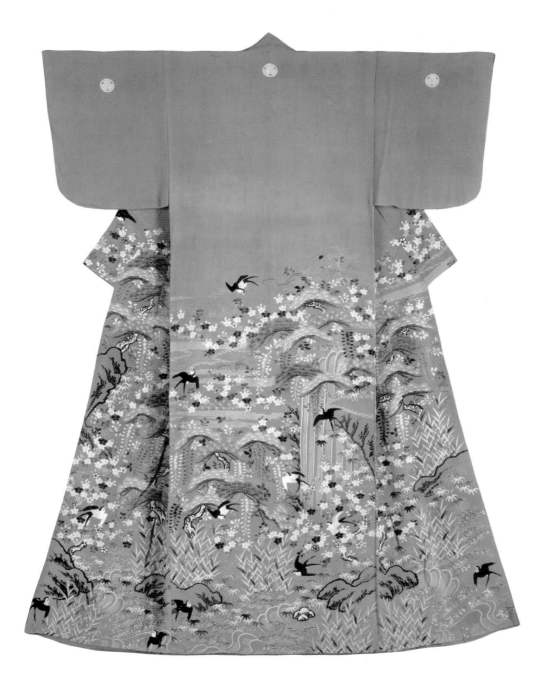

51

52   *Furisode* with Ancient Court Carriage, Pines, Maples,
Chrysanthemums, and Bush Clover

Dye and embroidery

Light blue *chirimen* (crepe)

Height: 164 cm.; *yuki* 60 cm.; sleeve length: 90 cm.; sleeve width: 30 cm.

Late Edo period, end of eighteenth to first half nineteenth century

---

The motifs of streams, chrysanthemums, pine trees, and bush clover are
designed in the customary style of *kosode* for members of the aristocracy.
The motifs are reserved in white with paste resist and are embroidered.
The abundant and striking use of the gold and color embroidery adds a
flamboyant quality. The *goshoguruma* (oxen-pulled carriages) and straw
hat on the lower skirt allude to the story of a handsome aristocrat,
Fukagusa-no-chūjō. He tragically died of a broken heart after having been
refused by Ono-no-komachi, a famous poetess of unparalleled beauty of the
early Heian period, whom he courted for more than ninety-nine evenings.

52

53   *Katabira* with Garden Scenery

Chaya dyeing and embroidery
White hemp
Height: 174 cm.; *yuki*: 61.5 cm.; sleeve length: 46 cm.; sleeve width: 31 cm.
Mid- to late Edo period, mid-eighteenth to early nineteenth century

The perspective of the scene on this *katabira* is from overhead. Through
the clouds one can see *shiorido* (doors made of branches), chrysanthemums, bush clover, plums, ivy, willows, gingkos, and Chinese bellflowers
over a stream. Pine needles are arranged within the cloud shapes. The
golden moon on the upper right sleeve shows that it is evening. The dyeing
is done solely by the immersion dyeing method in indigo blue, except for a
partial brush painting in indigo blue. The white areas of the motifs are all
resisted with paste from the surface. Fine lines of paste are applied to the
detailed parts of the motifs, such as the veins of the leaves and each flower
petal. The paste is applied also from the back to surround the motifs. To
attain the different shades of indigo, the areas are dipped again in the
indigo vat. At the end, embroidery in color and gold is added. This technique, generally called *chaya* dyeing, is a dyeing technique for *katabira*
worn between May and September by the women of a warrior's household
in the Edo period. It is said that a Kyoto dry goods dealer, Chaya
Shirojiro, invented this dyeing method, but there exists no definite proof.

53

54 *Katabira* with Bridges and Pine Trees

Shibori, embroidery, and dye
White hemp
Height: 133 cm.; *yuki*: 60 cm.; sleeve length: 42.5 cm.; sleeve width: 31.5 cm.
Mid-Edo period, mid-eighteenth century

Fig. 2

The design of this *katabira* is simple, with clear contrast between the motifs of pines on a seashore, bridges, and wave crests. The ground is dyed in black while the wave crests have been resisted in *kanoko shibori*; at the same time the land and the bridges have been resisted by some other method. The outlines are sharply defined with brush painting. Some of the pines are decorated with *surihitta* (stenciled *kanoko* dots), with *bengara* (Indian red), or *airō* (indigo wax). Other pines are embroidered in green and gold. The wood grain of the bridges is depicted by freehand brush painting. Gold couching is applied to the railings. The whole composition is based on the Genroku style, but the spirit of the middle years of the mid-Edo period is felt in the evenly distributed motifs and reduced flamboyance.

The unnatural discontinuity of the motifs is due to the remaking of the *kosode* in later years, when the skirt was shortened and the sleeves cut short. When the motifs are correctly aligned, it becomes obvious that both sleeves used to be one left sleeve. In other words, this *katabira* was originally a *furisode* (long-sleeved *kosode*) that sustained damage to the right sleeve; two shorter sleeves were fashioned from the intact left sleeve. The original *kosode*, shown restored in Fig. 2, had a design that was beautifully continuous from the sleeves to the body.

54

55   *Juban* with Scenes of Edo

Embroidery
Gray cotton
Height: 135 cm.; *yuki*: 62.5 cm.; sleeve length: 53 cm.; sleeve width: 31 cm.
Late Edo period, mid-nineteenth century

Fig. 3

This is a man's *juban*, or undergarment, with scenes of the city of Edo along the river Sumida embroidered on gray cotton. On the back, from the left to the right sleeve, the bustle of Sensoji temple and its Nakamise marketplace are depicted. Around the skirt, Echigoya (the former Mitsuko-shi department store), Ryogoku bridge, and a series of earthen storehouses are depicted along the river Sumida. From the breast to the front right sleeve the Edo castle is depicted, with a view of Mt. Fuji in the distance (Fig. 3). The big building of the Kaneiji temple in Ueno stands opposite the mountain on the front left sleeve. Satin stitch is the major embroidery technique used here.

On the lower end of the right overlap, the seal of the embroiderer's studio is stitched. The top character of the seal reads *shū* (literally, "embroidery"), which suggests that it was a studio for embroidery specialists. The lower letter is illegible, and the exact name of the studio cannot be identified.

Juban is a word derived from *gibao*, or the Portugese word *jubao*, and refers to the undergarment worn directly on the skin. Earlier, hemp fabric was used, but from the late Edo period, cotton *juban* such as this became popular. Since *juban* is an undergarment, the design is hidden under the *kimono*. To include such crafted decoration on an undergarment was the result of a sense of beauty called *iki*, which became fashionable during the late Edo period. *Iki* reflected the idea that real luxury was found in hidden places and did not consist of overt displays. This taste for hidden luxury prevailed partly in protest against the frequently issued sumptuary laws and partly in reaction to the excessive decoration that had set the standard of beauty of the mature culture of the mid-Edo period. By this time, from a historical point of view, the Japanese way of dressing was transformed from the stylistic beauty of premodern era to that of the modern era.

55

56   *Kosode* with Cranes, Turtles, Wild Oranges, and Ferns

Embroidery
White *nume* (satin)
Height: 161 cm.; *yuki*: 62 cm.; sleeve length: 45 cm.; sleeve width: 31.5 cm.
Latter half Edo period, mid-nineteenth century

Very auspicious motifs are composed in green, yellow-green, navy, and gold thread against the white *nume* satin of this *kosode*. Cloud shapes trimmed with bamboo-blind screens are scattered all over; water flows around the skirt. The meaning of the combined motifs of ferns, wild oranges, crested cranes, turtles, and flowing water is unclear. The frayed embroidery, especially the black threads, and damaged areas are conspicuous. The design of both sleeves ends abruptly. Originally this must have been a *furisode*.

56

57   *Furisode* with Falconry Scene

Embroidery
Purple *chirimen* (crepe)
Height: 172 cm.; *yuki*: 65 cm.; sleeve length: 100 cm.; sleeve width: 33 cm.
End Edo period to early Meiji period, latter half nineteenth century

---

The entire surface of this *furisode* is treated as one canvas, on which a
falconry scene is depicted richly. Over a high mountain, with clusters of
snow-covered pine trees and a rushing waterfall, some falcons pursue
flying cranes and pheasants, while others rest on pine branches. Hunting
paraphernalia, such as bows and arrows, dogs, hunting attire of *mukabaki*
(fur apron for horseback riding), *utsubo* (cases for arrows), and hats, are
symbolically depicted. The pine trees, waterfall, and wildflowers are reserved
white in paste resist against the purple background. The fall is painted
blue and colorful embroidery is added. Various embroidery techniques are
evident in addition to the common gold *koma* stitch. *Warinui* stitch was
used to depict flowers, and *sashinui* stitch was used to depict the hawks,
pheasants, hunting attire, and dogs. Together these techniques realistically
render the feathers, petals, and other features in three dimensions. The
large motifs on the skirt area become smaller as they ascend, indicative of
a calculated composition in perspective. The density of the allover design
of this *kosode* indicates it may have been made as a *uchikake* (outer robe).
But since *rinzu* (figured satin) usually is used for *uchikake*, and this
kosode is made of *chirimen* (crepe), it is more appropriate to consider this
garment to have been a *furisode*.

57

58   *Furisode* with *Shō-Chiku-Bai* (Pine-Bamboo-Plum Trees)
       and Flying Cranes

Kanoko *shibori*

Indigo blue *rinzu* (figured satin)

Height: 156.5 cm.; *yuki*: 61.5 cm.; sleeve length: 93 cm.; sleeve width: 31 cm.

Latter half Edo period, mid-nineteenth century

This is a *furisode* for a wedding, with pines, bamboo, and grafted plum
trees. As was mentioned before, *shō-chiku-bai* (pine-bamboo-plum trees)
is a popular auspicious motif. Cranes also are a popular auspicious motif
representing long life. The composition, which is revivalistic, was inspired
by a *hiinakata* (fashion book) of the mid-Edo period. The only technique
that is used to create this *furisode* is *kanoko shibori* (tie-dyed dots). Some
undissolved tying threads still remain. Although the ground is dyed in
indigo, it looks white from a distance because of the densely packed
kanoko dots. *Kosode* with *so-hitta shibori* (allover *kanoko shibori*), like
this one, came into fashion in the latter half of the Edo period. The creative process is so time-consuming and requires such highly advanced
shibori technique that only the *furisode* of the best quality were done in
so-hitta *shibori*. It is very strange that the design is discontinuous between
the sleeves and the body of this *kosode*, which was created only after
much arduous labor. Originally the motifs must have been completely
continuous. As a matter of fact, if the sleeves are exchanged and correctly
aligned, the natural flow of the motifs appears. It seems that in later years
the garment was carelessly remade.

58

59   *Kosode*, by Matsumura Goshun, with Stately Mansion in
Mountain Landscape

White plain-weave silk
Freehand painting
Height: 165 cm.; *yuki*: 60 cm.; sleeve length: 43 cm.; sleeve width: 32 cm.
Mid-Edo period, late eighteenth century

Matsumura Goshun (1752–1811) studied under Buson (1761–1784)
and mastered *haikai* (a style of poetry) and *nanga* (southern school of
Chinese painting). Goshun studied the realistic style as a private pupil of
Maruyama Ōkyo. Later, he became the founder of the Shijō school. This
kosode, designed by Goshun, depicts a stately Chinese mansion and
mountain landscape in ink and wash painting. Here, his technique shows
the strong influence of Buson and the *nanga* style, and expresses the qui-
etude of the awesome mountains very well. The area from the left to the
right sleeve is left undecorated and is separated from the other areas by
the line of the ridge. The landscape appears larger and larger as it
descends toward the skirt. This composition shows the artist's thorough
understanding of *kosode* design. The same quality is apparent in another
brush-painted *kosode*, with plum trees and undergrowth, in the Nomura
collection, which was painted by Sakai Hoitsu. This *kosode* bears the seal
"Goshun *sha*" ("sketched by Goshun") near the right neckband. From the
characteristics of that seal and his style, it is thought that the garment was
created when the arist was in his thirties, from 1781–1789. There is
another extant *kosode* painted in freehand by Goshun, a *kosode* of white
satin, with spearflowers in the snow. In that *kosode*, which is preserved in
the Rakuto Ihokan, the progress of his technique, from the mastery of the
nanga style to his own established style, is evident. Probably created in
Goshun's later years, it is an interesting contrast to this *kosode*.

59

60   *Furisode* with Bamboo Blind and Cypress-Slat Fans

Yūzen dyeing, *shibori*, and embroidery
Crimson *nume* silk,
Height: 170 cm.; *yuki*: 62 cm.; sleeve length: 101 cm.; sleeve width: 32.5 cm.
Latter half Edo period, mid-nineteenth century

Using the whole surface of the *kosode* as one canvas, the design of this
very luxurious *furisode* includes a *kichō* screen, which is visible among
the clouds through the blind on the upper half, and cypress-slat fans in
the lower half. The large screens and fan motifs are tied in *shibori*. At the
same time the auspicious cloud and diaper patterns of the seven-treasure
(*shippō-tsunagi*) motifs and *seikaiha* (wave crests in the blue ocean) are
tied in *kanoko shibori*. Then the ground is dyed in crimson *somewake*
(divided background). Auspicious and colorful motifs such as cranes, turtles, pines, bamboos, plums, wild oranges, and chrysanthemums are executed in *yūzen* to decorate the screen and fans. Rich embroidery in colored and gold thread are added to the outlines of the motifs and the
details of the decoration. There is another *furisode* with a white ground
and an identical design in the Nomura Collection; yet another *furisode*
with identical design, this one with a black ground, has been preserved
elsewhere. Originally these three *furisode* were one set of a wedding outfit
in which black, crimson, and white kimonos were worn in three layers.
White symbolized the purity of the bride. Crimson symbolized her loveli-
ness and beauty. Black expressed solemn and ceremonial feelings.

60

61   *Furisode* with Chrysanthemums and Fences

Yūzen dyeing and embroidery
Light blue *aya* (figured twill weave)
Height: 170.5 cm.; *yuki*: 62 cm.; sleeve length: 100 cm.; sleeve
width: 32.5 cm.
End Edo period to early Meiji period, latter half nineteenth century

Various kinds of hedges, such as *magaki* (rough woven bamboo fence),
shibagaki (brushwood fence), and *oriegaki* (woven twig fence), as well as
colorful chrysanthemums are rendered in *yūzen* and embroidery in this
furisode. Chrysanthemums, large and small, are depicted as if they were a
scene from one of the chrysanthemum exhibitions often held in Kyoto in
the early part of the eighteenth century. Bilateral symmetry is present in
this Edozuma design. The variety of the shapes of the fences and chrysanthemums, as well as the scattered chrysanthemum blossoms in the empty
spaces on the shoulders and around the waist, prevent the design from
becoming a cliché.

61

62   *Kosode* with Plum Trees and Spearflowers in Snow

Paste resist and embroidery
Light blue *rinzu* (figured satin)
Height: 155 cm.; *yuki*: 62.5 cm.; sleeve length: 51 cm.; sleeve width: 31.5 cm.
Meiji period, latter half nineteenth to early twentieth century

The *rinzu* material is woven with diaper patterns of *kikkō* (tortoise shell)
and wild orange motifs. The motifs have been reserved white in paste
resist, and the ground is dyed in light blue. Trees, snow, and spearflower
leaves are painted with pigment. The theme of the design is snow-covered
spearflowers and white-blossomed plum trees in early spring. *Tsukidashi*
technique, in which the material is poked with a stick from the back
to produce a projecting effect, is used in the plum blossoms. Crimson
embroidery is added only to the fruit of the spearflowers. The plum trees,
their bases sheltered from snow, stretch their trunks outward at the middle
of the overlap and spread their branches into the neckbands. The area
around the waist is left undecorated. The composition follows the bilateral symmetry common after the late Edo period. The design of the whole
kosode and the sharp-edged cuts of the sleeves resemble those of No. 63.
It is thought to have been made after the Meiji period.

62

63   *Kosode* with Spring Snow over Garden

Yūzen dyeing
Antwerp blue *chirimen* (crepe)
Height: 149 cm.; *yuki*: 62.5 cm.; sleeve length: 44 cm.; sleeve width: 31.5 cm.
Meiji period, latter half nineteenth to early twentieth century

A symmetrical composition unfolds in the area from the lower edge of the
left neckband to the lower edge of the right neckband. Between the pine
tree and the plum tree, which face each other, motifs of bamboo, daffo-
dils, a *shibagaki* (brushwood hedge), and a gate are depicted. The snow,
piled high in some areas, falls and settles on the trees, grass, and flowers; a
cold, crystal-clear stream flows among them. Since the Antwerp blue color
of the ground apparently symbolizes the night, the theme of this design
must be a garden on an early spring night. This is an elegant design, with
motifs reserved in white by paste resist, among which the stamens of the
blossoms, the leaves, and the tree bark are decorated by *yūzen* dyeing and
uwae (touch-up dyed figures). As is stated elsewhere, the combination of
pine, bamboo, and plum trees is one of the most popular auspicious
motifs in Japan. This *kosode* probably was worn on the festive occasions
related to the New Year. The symmetrical composition is in the tradition
of the customary style of the late Edo period, but the motifs, which are
more realistically expressed, and the sleeves, which are cut in acute angles,
are characteristic of the Meiji period.

63

64　*Furisode* with Chrysanthemums and Bamboo Fences
around Skirt

Yūzen dyeing
Light brown cotton
Height: 155.5 cm.; *yuki*: 62 cm.; sleeve length: 96 cm.; sleeve width: 31.5 cm.
End of Edo period to early Meiji period, latter half nineteenth century

Against the divided background, with a diaper pattern of *shohishi* (pine bark lozenges), motifs of clustered chrysanthemums on bamboo fences are designed in bilateral symmetry in the *Edozuma* style. Following the current fashion of the time the same chrysanthemum design is repeated on the lining of the skirt. The chrysanthemum motifs are simplified in the Kōrin style. They are brush-painted in light blue and brown, and white pigmented powder (*kofun*) is applied over them. The Kōrin style of the motifs shows a consistency and completeness distinct from earlier Kōrin designs, which lend a feeling of movement. This design has an effect similar to that of a black-and-white painting in that ink was used for the shades of the leaves against the ink-dyed background. Usually silk, especially *chirimen* (crepe), is used for *yūzen* dyeing, but hemp and cotton are also suitable. Very few examples of *yūzen*-dyed hemp and cotton dating from the modern age have been preserved, and this *furisode* is one of these rare examples.

64

65   *Furisode* with Cherry Trees and Pheasants

Cotton, *yūzen* dyeing
Light blue *nando* (gauze)
Height: 160 cm.; *yuki*: 58 cm.; sleeve length: 103 cm.; sleeve width: 29 cm.
Meiji period, latter half nineteenth to early twentieth century

This is a spring scene with cherry trees in full bloom, a couple of pheasants, reeds, milk vetch, and horsetails. Called a *tegaki* (handpainted) *yūzen*, this is an example of a *yūzen*-dyed cotton *furisode* similar to the *furisode* with chrysanthemums and bamboo fences of No. 64. After the motifs are resisted in paste, the ground is dyed blue. Then, painting in ink and various pigments is added. The design follows the standard of the latter half of the Edo period, in which the bilaterally symmetrical composition was placed on the lower edge of one neckband to the other, as well as on the lower sleeves, and continued to the skirt area of the lining. The pheasants, the major motif of the design, are placed on the lower left side of the skirt, which, when worn, is the front of the garment. Typical of the Meiji period is the realistic, pictorial design incorporated into the standard composition.

65

66   *Furisode* with Chrysanthemums and Small Bird in
Winter Scene

Yūzen dyeing with embroidery
Plain gray silk
Height: 155.5 cm.; *yuki*: 63 cm.; sleeve length: 96 cm.; sleeve
width: 32.5 cm.
Meiji period, latter half nineteenth to early twentieth century

---

Fig. 4

The slightly frozen pond in powdery falling snow is depicted in a simple
and sharp manner by the fine lines of the resist paste, while the snow-
covered earthen bank and the chrysanthemums are presented by paste
resist, brush painting with pigments, and embroidery with *nuikiri* and
sagara stitch. The small, quail-like bird on the earthen bank is embroidered in a realistic manner. The outside design is repeated on the lining of
the *kosode*, although the small bird is absent (Fig. 4). The cracked-ice
design is included in the *kosode* fashion books of the first half of the
eighteenth century. But in this design the geometric configuration of the
cracked ice, placed in juxtaposition to the snow-covered bank, is a very
realistic depiction. It recalls the depiction in *Hyōzu Byōbu* (*Screen with
Ice*) by Maruyama Ōkyo, which is preserved in the British Museum. The
most peculiar point of this design is that the snow-laden chrysanthemums
and the small bird are placed on the lower front flap of the *kosode*, which
is hidden when one gets dressed. After the middle years of the mid-Edo
period, in reaction to the decorativeness of the current culture, a new
sense of beauty favoring *teishi* was born. *Teishi* refers to the placing of
skillfully created images in hidden places so as not to render works of
only obvious beauty. As a result of *teishi*, the focus of *kosode* design gradually migrated to the lower skirt area, then to the skirt only, and finally to
the lining. This design intended to present *teishi*-style beauty, but it is a
peculiar one, nonetheless. The color of the ground and the somewhat
strange positioning of the motifs lend a very subdued impression to the
garment. Since it is a *furisode*, it must have been worn by a young woman.
It can be said that this is an extreme example of *teishi* in the Meiji period.

66

67   *Kosode* with Cherry Trees in Four Seasons

Yūzen dyeing with embroidery
Red purple *chirimen* (crepe)
Height: 161 cm.; *yuki*: 62.5 cm.; sleeve length: 46.5 cm.; sleeve width: 32.5 cm.
Latter half Edo period, mid-nineteenth century

Fig. 5

Cherry trees reflecting the four seasons are shown in full bloom, with green leaves, with tinted and fallen autumn leaves, and under a blanket of snow. The trees are displayed around the skirt, from the left to the right overlap hem (Fig. 5). The motifs are reserved in white by paste resist, and the leaves are depicted by *yūzen* dyeing. The hill and the trees are brush painted, and cherry blossoms are decorated with embroidery. The bilaterally symmetrical design, which is placed only around the skirt, reflects the tradition of the years after the mid-Edo period. The outside design is repeated on the skirt of the *kosode* lining. During the late Edo period, *iki* (understated chic) prevailed as a concept in *kosode* design. Another preference of the day—repeating on the inside of the robe the design decorating the outside, as in this case—came into fashion in later years, during the Bakumatsu (closing period of shogunal government) and the early Meiji period. This design can be described as intellectual in conception, but poetic in sentiment.

67

68   *Furisode* with Maple Trees, Curtain, and Drums

Yūzen dyeing with embroidery
Pale blue *aya* (figured twill weave)
Meiji period, late nineteenth to early twentieth century

Fig. 6

Clouds and maple trees spread above and below the waist, and curtains and a *dadaiko* (bass drum used for *bugaku*, the ancient court instrumental ensemble) fill the skirt. The clouds are dyed in crimson in *kanoko shibori* and stitch-resist *shibori*. Other motifs are freely rendered by *yūzen* dyeing. The technique is precise and the curtains are especially well defined. The last to be added is partial embroidery in color and in gold as well as outlines in ink. Gold *surihaku* (applied matallic leaf) is applied to the surrounding areas of the clouds. The patterns on the curtains read from left to right: peonies and vine scroll, *shō-chiku-bai* (pine-bamboo-plum), clouds, *takarazukushi* (figures symbolizing treasures such as health, worth, and comfort), thunderbolt crest, crane-in-lozenges, *kiku-sui* (chrysanthemums and flowing water), and *hatohorai* (waves from the Isle of Eternity).

The *dadaiko* (bass drum) is one of the auspicious motifs. The combination of maple trees and *dadaiko* is based on the "Koyonoga" ("Festival of Red Leaves") chapter of *The Tale of Genji*. In the autumn, at the musical performance for the occasion of the horseback viewing of the red maples in Seiryoden, Genji danced along with Tōno Chūjo, and enchanted the audience with his beauty. The motifs of the body and sleeves are not continuous or natural, due to later remaking. The original sleeve line is moved approximately 32 centimeters toward the front (Fig. 6). The original sleeve length was at least 104 centimeters, calculated from the present sleeve length of 72 centimeters plus 32 centimeters of the removed shoulder line; with its long sleeves, it belonged to the *furisode* category. From the length of the *furisode* sleeves and the content of the design, this kimono seems to have been used as the outer garment for a wedding kimono. The material is so-called *yatsuhashi*, a twill weave (*aya*) of 4/4 warp-weft structure, with a pattern of alternating squares and rectangles, which was in fashion from the Meiji to the Taishō period.

68

69   *Kosode* with Bats
          Yūzen and embroidery
          Reddish-brown *aya* (figured twill weave)
          Height: 165 cm.; *yuki*: 63 cm.; sleeve length: 44 cm.; sleeve width: 33 cm.
          Meiji period, late nineteenth to early twentieth century

---

With the same figured twill in the *yatsuhashi* pattern as in No. 68, this *kosode* is designed in the so-called *Edozuma* style, with a bilaterally symmetrical composition of bats, from the edges of both neckbands to the area very near the edge of the skirt. The bats are *yūzen* dyed in black and blue. Some bats are outlined with tightly twisted green or gold threads in *koma* stitch embroidery; others have compressed outlines or ears with plain black thread. Still others have gold painting added to their ears. The variety of the bats breaks the monotony of the design. Since bats are nocturnal animals that prefer darkness, they are considered ominous in the West. But because the Chinese character of the second letter of the word *komori* (bats), which also can be read *fuku*, is homophonic to the second letter of the word *kofuku*, which means *happiness*, bats have been treated as an auspicious motif in China. In Japan, bats were thought to be eerie creatures and seldom were adopted as a motif. But as the latter half of the Edo period approached, the intentional seeking of peculiar motifs, called *iki*, came into fashion. The quality of the material indicates that this *kosode* dates from the Meiji period, but it is an example which still strongly conforms to the *iki* taste of the Edo period.

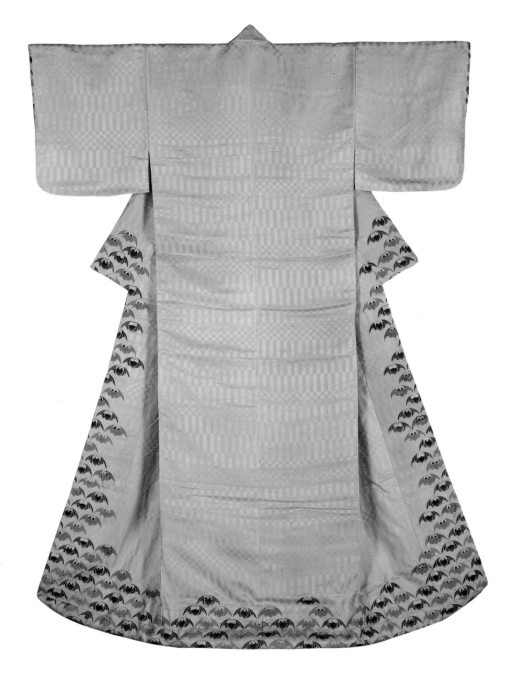

69

70   *Kosode* with Playing Puppies and Flowering Weeds

Light brown *chirimen* (crepe)
Dye and embroidery
Height: 156.5 cm.; *yuki*: 62 cm.; sleeve length: 45 cm.; sleeve
width: 32 cm.
Late Meiji to early Taishō period, early half twentieth century

This *Edozuma* design shows a spring field in which puppies play among
such flowering weeds as dandelions, violets, and Chinese milk vetch. The
puppies are embroidered; the flowers are reserved in white with paste
resist and embroidered at the end. Like No. 69, this is another example of
a design with strange motifs. The characteristics of the Edo period already
are lost; the *kosode* probably was made at the end of the Meiji period
(1868–1912) or possibly during the Taishō period.

70

71   *Kosode* with Ikat Patterned with Arrow Shapes,
      Chrysanthemums, Maples, and Plum Branches

Embroidery
Silk *ikat*
Height: 156 cm.; *yuki*: 60 cm.; sleeve length: 44 cm.; sleeve width: 31 cm.
Meiji period, latter half nineteenth to early twentieth century

On purple ikat patterned with arrow shapes, motifs of chrysanthemums
and broken branches of maple and plum trees are embroidered in a scattered manner. Embroidering the floral motifs in brightly colored thread,
threads so bright that they give the impression that synthetic dyes were
used, is a characteristic of *kosode* worn by aristocratic women from the
end of the Edo period to the Meiji period. Since ikat patterned with arrow
shapes was seldom used as a background material, this *kosode* is a particularly rare one. Ikat is a general name for weavings made with silk threads
dyed at even intervals and woven into a pattern. *Yagasuri* is a kind of ikat
that is woven with dyed threads twisted at even intervals for the weft,
which is then woven so that an arrow-shaped pattern results. Ikat was
popular among the merchant class in the Edo period, but was seldom
used among the aristocrats and the warrior class. Minute-patterned arrow
feathers were fashionable for a period during the Meiji era. Whether or
not this *kosode* dates from that period is one of many unanswered questions this garment raises.

71

202

72   Unlined *Kosode* with Flowing Water, Autumn
      Wildflowers, and Flying Wild Geese

Embroidery
Purple *rō* (silk gauze)
Height: 161.5 cm.; *yuki*: 62 cm.; sleeve length: 45 cm.; sleeve
width: 31.5 cm.
Meiji period, latter half nineteenth to early twentieth century

---

This colorfully embroidered summer *kosode* depicts a stream and wildflowers blooming in profusion on the banks. The autumn flowers on the
banks include chrysanthemums, bellflowers, eularias, bush clover, yellow
valerian, and ivy. On the upper back and front the crimson autumn leaves
of the far mountains and alighting wild geese are visible among the
clouds, which are decorated with gold couching. The flowing water and
other motifs project a visual coolness in a *kosode* decorated with embroidery alone. This *kosode* was probably worn by a warrior-class woman of
the Tokugawa shogunate or the early Meiji period.

73	*Katabira* with Wisteria and Peony Fences

Embroidery and *shibori*
Black hemp
Height: 171 cm.; *yuki*: 62 cm.; sleeve length: 44 cm.; sleeve width: 32 cm.
End Edo period to Meiji period, latter half nineteenth to early twentieth century

---

The abundant wisteria, peonies, and meadowsweet of early summer are depicted in embroidery and paste resist against a black hemp ground in this tidy *katabira*. From the sleeves to the body, clouds and wisteria are reserved in white in fine lines of resist paste against a black background. The vines and leaves of the wisteria are embroidered in bright light green and light yellow-green thread through the use of such techniques as *matsui*, *nuikiri*, and *norikake* stitch. Red and white peonies and meadow-sweet, with fences and undergrowth, spread under the waist of the full skirt of this garment. The fences are executed in gold *koma* stitch. The tying threads at the joints of the fences are embroidered in crimson thread. The brightly colored embroidery threads are thought to have been syn-thetically dyed. This design is similar to that of the *katabira* in No. 71. It is considered to be a summer garment worn by an aristocratic woman around the end of the Edo period to the Meiji period.

73

Furisode with Flowing Water and Flowers

Yūzen dyeing
Light blue *rō chirimen* (silk gauze crepe)
Height: 158 cm.; *yuki*: 60 cm.; sleeve length: 100 cm.; sleeve width: 33 cm.
End Meiji period, early twentieth century

This *furisode* and the one in No. 75 belonged to Lady Mieko, a member
of the Imperial Arisugawa family. In 1908, she married Yoshihisa, a son of
the last shogun, Yoshinobu, of the Tokugawa government. The design is
composed in the bilateral symmetry of the *Edozuma* style, with pinks,
mallows, and cherry blossoms over a background of water. Since the
material is *rō* (silk gauze weave alternating with plain weave), this *furisode*
would have been worn during summer. The primary decorative technique
used is *yūzen* dyeing, with the outlines of the flowers and leaves defined in
gold paint and with embroidery added. This *furisode*, actually worn by an
aristocrat at the end of the Meiji period, is a very important piece offering
information about the status of comtemporary *yūzen* dyeing at its best.

Compared with previous examples, this *yūzen*-dyed *furisode* shows different hues because all the dyes used are synthetic. It was around 1862 that
synthetic dyes were first imported to Japan, and the use of them spread
rapidly during the Meiji period since they were much easier to handle and
thus were more convenient to use than natural dyes. Synthetic dyes that
can render freely various colors greatly influenced *yūzen* dyeing. Most
significantly, *hikizome* (brush painting of the entire piece of material) was
made possible in any color. As was stated several times earlier, only natural dyes were used in *yūzen* dyeing of the Edo period. If a dye, such as
indigo blue, was not suitable for *hikizome* the ground was dyed by immersion; however, immersion dyeing of the ground complicated the *yūzen*
process and required the talents of only the most expert craftsmen. That
changed with the introduction of synthetic dyes, at which point the
ground could be dyed in a favorite color simultaneously with *irosashi*
(brush painting) of the motifs. The use of the synthetic dyes made *yūzen*
dyeing more colorful and more available to the general public. Although
most traditional dyeing techniques are declining in popularity, *yūzen* still
retains its prominence.

74

75   *Furisode* with Flowing Water and Autumn Flowers

Purple *chirimen* (crepe)

Yūzen dyeing

Height: 162.5 cm.; *yuki*: 65 cm.; sleeve length: 102 cm.; sleeve width: 34 cm.

Late Meiji period, early twentieth century

Like No. 74, this *furisode* was worn by Tokugawa Mieko. Motifs of autumn flowers, such as pinks, cotton roses, Chinese bellflowers, bush clover, and chrysanthemums over a pattern of flowing water, are composed in bilateral symmetry, spreading from both sleeves to cover the skirt. The applied technique is *yūzen* dyeing. Synthetic dyes are used both in the brush painting and the dyeing of the ground, which lend a highly realistic and glossy appearance to this design.

75

76   Kimono with Autumn Grass

Inagaki Toshijiro (1902–1963)
Katazome (stencil dyeing)
Tsumugi (spun-floss silk)
Height: 152 cm.; width: 136 cm.
1961

Resist paste is applied through paper patterns to stencil-dye this kimono. Among the traditional and professionalized stencil dyeing techniques, *komon*, *chūgata*, *kata-yūzen*, and *bingata* are especially well known. A new style of stencil dyeing, in which paper patterns are used freely without any of the traditional restrictions, has been created by a few contemporary artists. This new style is sometimes called *katazome*.

The maker of this kimono was the second son of an artist who specialized in traditional Japanese painting. After graduating from the design department of the City Technological School of Kyoto, he came to be in charge of *kata-yūzen* designs in the garment design department of a department store, where he worked for about ten years. The first publicized art kimonos that he created as an independent artist were decorated by freehand painting. Later, he adopted stencil dyeing. His stencil-dyed works were highly praised, and he was conferred the title of "Possessor of an Important Intangible Cultural Asset" by the government in 1962.

The motifs he frequently used were taken primarily from common scenes and annual events of Kyoto. The motif of certain weeds (*inutade*) in this kimono was one of his favorite plant motifs. The dyes used were *momokawa* brown, yellow, indigo blue, and *sohō* (Indian red). This kimono, which expresses the atmosphere of the autumn season in Kyoto particularly well, was favorably received.

76

77   Kimono: *Danryū* (A Warm Current)

Ogura Kensuke (1897–1982)
Shibori dyeing
Chirimen (crepe)
Height: 145 cm.; width: 126 cm.
1960

In the title of this *shibori*-dyed work, *danryū* refers to an ocean full of fish. The wide stripes of the currents are executed in oke (vat) dyeing. The fish are executed in *hitome shibori* and *saka bōshi* (upside-down capped) *shibori*. At *Arimatsu Narutokai Shibori*, one of the famous *shibori* production centers in Japan, nearly fifty kinds of *shibori* dyeing techniques are exercised. The artist mastered his *shibori* techniques at this production center.

The artist was born in Miyazu city. At the age of sixteen he became a private apprentice of Ogura Manjirō in Kyoto. While working in the master's *yūzen* studio, he studied *shibori* dyeing. The well-known Japanese Traditional Craft Exhibition was inaugurated in 1955, but it was not until later that Ogura Kensuke participated in the exhibition. When he was sixty-one years old, he submitted his *shibori* works for the first time. He was held in great esteem for his use of *shibori* dyeing in kimono art. It is said that his interest in creating *shibori*-dyed kimonos was the result of his having been very moved by *tsujigahana* design, an important tradition in the Japanese textile history to which he had been exposed during his youth.

77

78   Kimono with Mallows

Kimura Uzan (1891−1977)
Freehand painting and *yūzen* dyeing
Chirimen (crepe)
Height: 166 cm.; width: 128
1971

In *yūzen* dyeing, resist paste is squeezed from the tip of a narrow tube onto the ground and the dye is then hand painted with a large brush. The flexibility in depiction, which is evident in this kimono, is one of the characteristics of *yūzen* dyeing. The cities of Kyoto, Kanazawa, and Tokyo are three major production centers for *yūzen* dyeing.

The artist, born in Kanazawa, gained fame as a *yūzen* artist in Kanazawa. At the age of fourteen, he recieved training in *yūzen* techniques and Japanese painting. The *yūzen* tradition in Kanazawa was in a state of decline during the time that he was mastering the technique. It is said that Kimura himself did not know what the *yūzen* tradition was. He developed his own designs based on his conception of the natural world. His creativity greatly influenced the textile work of Kanazawa during that time. *Yūzen* technicians were merely mechanically imitating old *yūzen* designs whose liveliness had been lost, but under Kimura's influence and leadership, the *yūzen* works of Kanazawa have come to be loved by the contemporary public once again. Kimura was conferred the title "Possessor of an Important Intangible Cultural Asset" by the government in 1955.

78

79　　Edo *Komon* Kimono: *Nashi no Kirikuchi*
　　　 (A Section of a Pear)

Komiya Yasutaka (born 1927)

Komon katazome

Chirimen (crepe)

1979

This kimono is dyed using the *komon* dyeing technique in which resist paste is applied through the *komon* (literally, "minute motifs") stencil before the ground is dyed. For this kimono a single *komon* pattern, approximately 35.5 x 15.2 centimeters, is used repeatedly to stencil the entire piece of material, which is approximately 4.3 × 9.9 meters. The stencil is made of Japanese paper that has been treated in persimmon tannin. The design of the pattern is then cut into the treated paper with a sculpting knife. A group of professional sculptors using this technique has kept the tradition alive in Suzuka city in the Mie prefecture until the present day. Komiya Yasutaka is a dyeing craftsman who has liked to use the patterns produced by this group.

Throughout the Edo period, *komon* was in large demand by the Daimyos and other warriors for the designs of the *hakama* (pleated skirt). Since the Meiji Restoration when the warrior class was disbanded by law, *komon* has come to be popular as one of the dye patterns of women's kimonos. Dyeing in a single color is one of the major characteristics of *komon*. It is especially loved in the Tokyo area. Hand-dyed *komon* is rarely seen today, but members of the Komiya family, including Yasusuke, Yasutaka, and Yasumasa, have maintained that tradition for more than three generations. The late Komiya Yasusuke was designated as a "Possessor of an Important Intangible Cultural Asset" by the government in 1955. Komiya Yasutaka also received that honor in 1978.

80　Woodprint Kimono

Koyama Yasuie (born 1903)
Woodprint
Chirimen (crepe)
Height: 171 cm.; width: 130 cm.
1969

The design depicts flying birds. In this technique dyes are pressed firmly onto the material with several kinds of small wood blocks. This technique was first developed by the artist in 1953. Koyama Yasui has come to be known as a woodprint artist since he started to send his works to the Japanese Traditional Craft Exhibition. The technique described above was inspired by a long-dead tradition of motif dyeing techniques using engraved wood blocks. Between 1955 and 1965, there appeared many artists like Koyama who interpreted historical techniques in a new way. The potential for expression in kimono designs was changed drastically by these artists.

Koyama Yasuie first studied Japanese painting. Later, he started to work with such dyeing techniques as *yūzen* and *katazome* (stencil dyeing), eventually working in woodprint. He is still active in Tokyo.

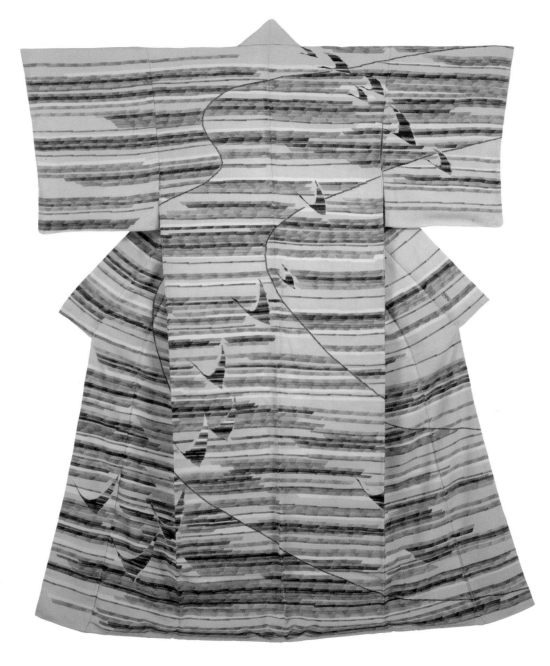

80

81   *Yokui* (Bathrobe) with Bamboo Pattern

Shimizu Kōtarō (born 1897)
Nagaita chūgata
Cotton
Height: 153 cm.; width: 126 cm.
1965

A *chūgata* paper stencil is used in dyeing this *yokui* (bathrobe). The
chūgata technique has been used mostly for dyeing bathrobes since the
Meiji period. In this technique exactly the same motifs are dyed in indigo
on both the front and back of the kimono. During the Bakumatsu (closing
period of the Edo shogunal government) and the Meiji period, kimonos
were produced in Tokyo with very precise *chūgata* techniques. The
nimaigata technique, in which two patterns were combined to create one
design, was applied to the high quality kimonos in limited numbers. The
combination of two patterns of *nimaigata* was substituted by a single new,
simpler pattern in 1930; however, a few craftsmen have kept the original
nimaigata technique alive until today.

Shimizu Kōtarō is one of those few craftsmen. When he was fourteen, he
received training from his father in *chūgata* stencil dyeing. He became
known as an excellent technician in the field at an early age. He was designated a "Possessor of an Important Intangible Cultural Asset" by the
government in 1955. It had not been customary for a traditional craftsman such as he to submit works to exhibitions as an artist. But since the
institution of the Possessor of an Important Intangible Cultural Assets
was established, works by the traditional craftsmen-artists have been
introduced in the Japanese Traditional Craft Exhibition. As the exhibition
has increased in fame, it has received positive acclaim from the press, and
these artists have come to be recognized as professional craftsmen-artists.

81

82   *Tsumugi* Kimono: *Hashigakari*
        (A Nō Bridge-form Passageway)

        Shimura Fukumi (born 1924)
        Plant dyes
        Tsumugi (spun floss plain-weave silk)
        Height: 166 cm.; width: 134 cm.
        1978

Tsumugi is a weave using threads spun from floss. *Tsumugi* techniques
have been passed down within families and are used to produce woven
clothing in households in all parts of Japan. The weave pattern of *tsumugi*
is a basic simple weave (*hiraori*). Traditionally only stripes or ikat were
used for decoration, but the artist has discovered new possibilities of
expression in *tsumugi* weave patterns. Between 1955 and 1965 her free
decorations, which were made of a combination of various colored threads
that she herself dyed in plant dyes, drew public attention. Because of their
unprecedented brightness and expressiveness, her *tsumugi* works became
a new fashion. The title of this kimono, *Hashigakari*, actually is taken
from a part of Nō theatre construction. The artist's original creations find
their inspiration in the images of Japanese classic literature.

Shimura Fukumi started studying weaving when she was thirty-one years
old. She received an award in the Japanese Traditional Craft Exhibition
after two years and received awards in the three consecutive years after
that. She is also known for her recent essays on weaves. Many young people have come to adore *tsumugi* through Shimura's works. Shimura teaches
pupils who live and work in a studio in her house.

82

83   Woodprint Kimono with Pine Pattern

Suzuta Teruji (1916–1981)
Woodprint
Tsumugi (spun floss plain-weave silk)
Height: 168 cm.; width: 134 cm.
1972

Pine needles are made into patterns in this work of *tsumugi* weave. Both the dyeing technique, in which the pigments are pressed on the material with the engraved wood blocks, and the stencil dyeing, which uses paper stencils, are applied to execute this design. The combination of the two dyeing techniques is based on the traditional technique of *Nabeshima sarasa*, which was practiced in the artist's home, Saga, where the Nabeshima clan lived. *Nabeshima sarasa* was developed from *sarasa* (Indian or Indonesian prints) which were imported during the Momoyama period. The techniques of the time, Japanese woodprinting and stencil dyeing, were applied to imitate the patterns of the imported *sarasa*. Throughout the Edo period, along with *Iro Nabeshima* and *Nabeshima dantsu* (carpets), *Nabeshima sarasa* was protected by law in the studios run by the Nabeshima clan government itself. During the time between the abolition of the clan system and the adoption of the prefecture system at the end of the Meiji period, the technicians who had worked in the clan studios disappeared and the technique was lost. However, some documents that recorded the technique were discovered. The artist studied the documents and restored the technique.

Suzuta Teruji was born in Saga prefecture. He was a graduate of the design department of the Tokyo Advanced School of Technology. At first he made works by wax dyeing. From 1950 he studied stencil-pattern dyeing under Inagaki, Nenjirō, and was active in stencil dyeing for about twenty years. During these years he continued his study of *Nabeshima sarasa*, and made study trips to Indonesia, Ceylon, and India. He began making his woodprint works public in 1972.

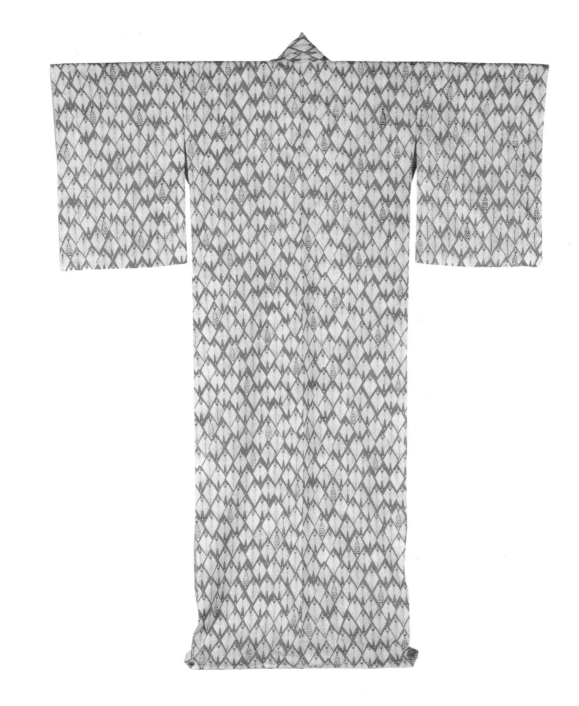

83

84 *Katazome* Kimono with Flowers and Birds

Serizawa Keisuke (1895–1984)
Stencil-pattern dyeing (*katazome*)
Bashōfu (abaca cloth)
Height: 145 cm.; width: 124 cm.
1959

This is a stencil-pattern dyed work on abaca cloth from Okinawa. The artist's stencil-dyeing technique was acquired by studying *bingata*, a traditional dyeing method of Okinawa, and so-called country stenciling, which had been practiced in all parts of Japan. His technique was similar to *chūgata*, with an especially significant difference; the techniques of *chūgata*, popular in urban areas, were so refined that the processes of making the patterns, stenciling, and dyeing were each executed by different specialists, but this artist carried out all the processes himself.

Serizawa Keisuke was born in Shizuoka prefecture. In 1916, he was enrolled in the design department of the Tokyo Advanced Technological School, specializing in the area of print designs After graduating from this school, he began work as a designer in Shizuoka. At the age of thirty, he came under the influence of Ryū Sōetsu and his theory on ethnic crafts. It was Ryū who encouraged him to start stencil dyeing. Although, generally, Japanese traditional craftsmen limited their work to their areas of specialty, Serizawa produced a very wide range of work. While limiting himself to stenciling works, he participated in creating picture books, kimonos, *noren* curtains, *futon* mat covers, screens, hanging scrolls, book illustrations, and calendars.

He also was actively involved in interior design, furniture design, and signage. He was designated a "Possessor of an Important Intangible Cultural Asset" in 1956. In 1976 he was honored for his distinguished services to Japanese culture (Bunka Kōrōsha). The term *kataezome* was associated with his type of work when he was designated a "Possessor of an Intangible Cultural Asset." The permanent collection of Serizawa's works are exhibited in the Serizawa Museum of the Ōhara Museum, the Sunagawa Art and Craft Museum, and the Shizuoka City Museum of Serizawa Keisuke Works.

84

85   Kimono with Diaper Patterns

Serizawa Keisuke (1895–1984)
Bashōfu (abaca cloth)
Katazome (stencil dyeing)
Height: 128 cm.; width: 124 cm.
1959

Decorative motifs are applied to dyed material. The original motifs, which the artist created, seem to posses the power to evoke a nostalgic feeling about the good old days, which lies deep within the hearts of the Japanese. One reason behind this apparent power stems from the fact that the objects he transformed into motifs were things that were a part of everyday life or the familiar scenes from the home country; another reason is that *katazome* technique itself is extremely familiar to the Japanese.

85

86   Kimono: *You-ei* (Swaying Shadows)

Tajima, Hiroshi (born 1922)
Freehand painting *yūzen* dyeing
Chirimen (crepe)
Height: 160 cm.; width: 124 cm.
1960

Swaying shadows reflected on the water are portrayed on this kimono. The *sekidashi* (sheeting) technique of *yūzen* dyeing is used to create this design. In *yūzen* dyeing there are two major techniques: freehand painting *yūzen* and *kata* (stencil) *yūzen*. In addition, there are two methods of free-hand painting *yūzen* dyeing: *itome* (fine-line) *yūzen* and *sekidashi* (sheeting) *yūzen*. *Itome yūzen* is one of the basic techniques of *yūzen* dyeing, in which resist paste is applied over the outlines of the motifs before the color is added. In *sekidashi yūzen* the coloring and the application of the resist-paste processes are repeated to eliminate the fine lines. A pictorial touch and coloring are characteristics of this *sekidashi* method, of which Tajima is a master.

Tajima Hiroshi was born in Tokyo. At the age of fourteen, he began his study of *yūzen* dyeing. His works were accepted for the first time in the Japanese Traditional Craft Exhibition of 1956. He received several awards and has become known as an artist whose works are in a style that reflects the taste of Tokyo residents. Presently he is considered one of the most established artists because of his techniques and design ideas.

86

87   Kimono with Clouds

Nakamura Katsuma (1894–1982)
Freehand painting *yūzen* dyeing
Black *chirimen* (crepe)
Height: 156 cm.; width: 126 cm.
1958

Flying clouds blown by the wind are depicted on a *chirimen* (crepe) ground. The ground is dyed black according to the custom of married women's formal kimonos, which are called *kuro* (black) *tomesode*. The design of black formal kimono is said to have remained strictly traditional compared to other robe designs. Dye artists seldom send their black formal kimonos to public exhibitions, probably because of the many restrictions on the designs of this formal wear. Nakamura Katsuma was the only artist who made an effort to incorporate new spirit into the designs of black kimono.

A dyeing technique called *musen* (no-line) *yūzen* was used to create this kimono. In this method mordants are applied directly to the ground. Before the mordants have dried, motifs are hand painted in dye. The name *musen* stems from an avoidance of the fine lines of paste. *Musen yūzen* had been experimented with and practiced for some time during the 1900s. Because it was a simple method, it was considered a low-quality dyeing technique. The artist has stated somewhere that in order to shed old feelings that clung to formal kimono designs, he went to the trouble of using this method, which had seldom been practiced at the time, in this work. When it was publicized, this kimono was praised in art magazines for its fresh spirit.

Nakamura Katsuma was born in Hakodate City. At the age of eighteen he came to Tokyo to attend Kawabata Painting School to study Japanese painting, but dropped out. He became a private pupil of a dyeing artist and mastered design and dyeing. Later, he worked as an artist in a large department store and specialized in the dyeing of high-quality kimonos. He was designated a "Possessor of an Important Intangible Cultural Asset" in 1955.

87

88   Kimono: *Taishun* (Waiting for the Spring)

Munehiro Rikizō (born 1914)
Ikat dyeing
Spun floss simple-weave silk
Height: 156 cm.; width: 124 cm.
1963

This kimono is made of a *tsumugi* weave of spun floss. The ikat dyeing
and weave pattern of this kimono is so-called *zurashi kasuri* (sliding ikat),
which is one of the rustic techniques. In this method the weft, which is
dyed in different colors, literally is slid to achieve the pattern. Using this
technique the artist renders curved lines and circles. Such patterns, the
likes of which have seldom been seen in the traditional ikat designs, were
originated by Munehiro.

After World War II, the artist made up his mind to go back to his home in
a deserted village in Gujō Hachiman, Gujō district, in Gifu prefecture, to
start a hand-weave industry. The tradition of *tsumugi* in Gujō Hachiman
was barely surviving, and he tried improve it by importing and raising a
special variety of silkworm from the Assam district of India. He improved
the quality of silk thread produced from these silkworms while he studied
ways to dye the threads. His effort to increase the value of the thread as
merchandise was successful. While he was working as a businessman, he
also set up exhibitions to bring local industry to the attention of a wider
public. He included ikat dyeing in the industry in response to market
demand. Since 1965, he has sent the results of his experiments with this
ikat weave to the Japanese Traditional Craft Exhibition. His new design of
ikat, which had never been seen before, and his careful manner of dyeing
drew new, enthusiastic customers. On a continuing basis, several trainees
receive instruction in weave techniques from Munehiro at his studio.
Today, more than 300 people have graduated from his studio and are
working in the weaving field in all parts of Japan. He was designated a
"Possessor of an Important Intangible Cultural Asset" in 1977. Because
of health problems he has moved his studio from Gujō Hachiman to
Minami-Ashigara City in Kanagawa prefecture.

88

89   Kimono: *Kiku* (Chrysanthemum)

Moriguchi Kakō (born 1909)
Freehand painting *yūzen* dyeing
Chirimen (crepe)
Height: 168 cm.; width: 126 cm.
1970

One chrysanthemum plant decorates this kimono. Along with the authentic *itome* (fine-line) *yūzen* technique, other *yūzen* techniques of *sekidashi* (sheeting) and *makinori* (scattered paste) are applied. The *makinori* technique produces an effect similar to *nashikoji* (pear-ground) in lacquer crafts, which can be seen in the depiction of the leaves. In the *makinori* technique, which is the artist's invention, resist paste is broken and the broken pieces are scattered and stuck to the ground before it is dyed. The dye used to depict the design is ink on black ground. The yellow of the chrysanthemum petals is derived from onion skin juice. The composition is intended to achieve a rhythmical beauty when the kimono is worn. Moriguchi is known as one of the top artists in expressing rhythmical movement in his designs and for his abundant *yūzen* designs.

Moriguchi Kakō was born in Shiga prefecture. His real name was Heishichiro, but he was given the pen name of Kakō when he became an independent *yūzen* master. At the age of fifteen he became a disciple of a *yūzen* master in Kyoto. In 1955 he sent his works to the Japanese Traditional Craft Exhibition and has since distinguished himself as a new leader in *yūzen* dyeing. At the 1955 exhibition, his first exhibition opportunity, he submitted three works: one created in a style in common practice, a second work created in an experimental style, and a third work which stood in between the first two in style. Among these three works the second work, the one in the experimental style, was received with high regard, and he subsequently developed a fine reputation. This reputation grew in part as a result of his eager pursuit of his own artistic sense, which separated his designs from the common ones required by commission agents, and also from the freshness of expression attained by his original *makinori* dyeing technique. Through his works he greatly influenced the world of contemporary *yūzen*, which had been stagnating.
He was designated a "Possessor of an Important Intangible Cultural Asset" in 1967.

89

90   Kimono: *Yūnagi* (An Evening Calm)

Yamada Mitsugi (born 1912)
Freehand painting *yūzen* dyeing
Tsumugi (spun floss silk)
Height: 166 cm.; width: 136 cm.
1978

Fishnets hanging out to dry on the beach are depicted in this kimono. The indigo blue color of the ground suggests the calm hours of evening. Discarding the fixed idea that *yūzen* dyeing employs a variety of colors, the artist reduced the numbers of colors; only the shades of indigo blue are used here. The *itome* (fine-line) *yūzen* technique is fully utilized in the net motif.

The artist was born in Gifu city. At the age of fifteen, he became a private pupil of Nakamura Katsuma to study *yūzen* dyeing. He began sending his works to the Japanese Traditional Craft Exhibition in 1958. Yamada Mitsugi has been cultivating the *yūzen* style in "Tokyo taste," in which the dexterity of the technique is pursued in designs which appear abstract at first glance. He was designated a "Possessor of an Important Intangible Cultural Asset" in 1985.

90

Glossary

Weave Structures

AYA-ORI: Twill weave. The weft yarn crosses over or under three or more warp yarns in twill weaves. The point where the weft and warp cross is called the *soshikiten*, or structure point. In a twill weave the structure point floats successively to create a diagonal pattern on the surface of the fabric.

HIRA-ORI: Plain weave. Among the three basic weave structures, *hira-ori* is the simplest. The weft and warp are alternately crossed.

SHUSU-ORI: Satin weave. The structure point in *shusu* weave does not float successively but intermittently. The float is so long that it looks as if only the warp or the weft was used. The surface is shiny and smooth.

Fabrics

CHIRIMEN: Textured silk crepe. Produced by simple weave (*hira-ori*) of untwisted (*hira-kiito*) warps and highly twisted wefts, whose twist direction alternates. The tension between the warps and wefts in different directions causes a ribbed surface. It is said that during the Tensho years (1573–1592), a weave craftsman came from China and taught the technique in Sakai, Japan. Favored ground for *yūzen* dyeing.

DONSU: Damask. A silk weave of satin structure. Different from *rinzu* in that its silk threads are refined and dyed prior to weaving and it is reversible with patterns on both sides.

NANAGO: Satin. A variation of *hira-ori* (plain weave) with a set of two warps and two wefts. The fine stone pavement pattern resembles fish eggs, after which the weave is named. *Nanago*, translated literally from the Chinese characters, means *fish-fish-child*.

NERINUKI: A plain weave (*hira-ori*) of unglossed silk (*kiito*) warps and glossed silk (*neriito*) wefts. It has a distinctive tension and luster and is favored in *tsujigahana* designs. In the Edo period it was used for *koshimaki* robes. It lost its popularity after *rinzu* appeared.

NUME: Unfigured satin. The ground is of a thin satin structure with a smooth, lustrous surface. It is sometimes used in place of *e-kinu* (a plain weave with unglossed and even silk warps and wefts) for paintings.

RINZU: Figured satin. The ground is a satin structure, and the pattern is produced in a backside satin structure. Unglossed silk (*kiito*) is used at the time of weaving. After it is woven it is refined, the excess fat and other impurities removed. A *sayagata* (key-fret) pattern with orchids and chrysanthemums is often used. This is a good fabric for dyeing. Throughout the Edo period it was used for high quality *kosode*.

RŌ: Gauze weave alternating with plain weave. A warp yarn crosses three, five, or seven weft yarns in the plain weave, and the two warp yarns are twisted. Softer and more pliable than *sha* (gauze weave), *rō* was popular for summer *kosode* during the Edo period and remains in use today.

Decorative Techniques

BŌSHI-SHIBORI: A technique in which outlines of motifs to be reserved are sewn and the thread pulled tightly so that the center of the motifs projects. Then the motifs are capped for resist in bamboo sheaths or oilpaper and immersion dyed.

HIKI-ZOME: A technique in which dye or pigment is applied to fabric by brush, as opposed to immersion dyeing. Used in *yūzen* dyeing.

HIRA-NUI: *See* NUIKIRI.

IKAT: A method of creating a reserved pattern by tie dyeing warp and/or weft before weaving. The work is of Malaysian origin and in Japan is known as *kasuri*.

KAGE-NUI: Hidden stitch. An embroidery technique which involves outlining the motifs without filling the surface of the motifs. Used regularly in floral motifs in *kosode* in the Genroku style.

KANOKO-SHIBORI: A technique in which very small portions of the fabric are compressed and tied with a thread for resist before immersion dyeing. The resulting pattern of dots, which resembles the white spots of a fawn, is called *kanoko* (deer).

KOMA-NUI: Couching. Colored, gold, and silver threads that are too thick to pass through the eye of a needle are laid along the underdrawing and couched by another thin silk thread. *Koma* is the general term for the spools used for these thick threads.

MATSUI-NUI: An embroidery technique for rendering lines. The curved stitch follows upward the lines of the underdrawing and the width of the lines are varied by the layers of the stitch.

NORIKAKE-NUI: Restitching undertaken in order to hold down long floats.

NUIHAKU: A combined technique of embroidery and *surihaku* (applied metallic leaf). Also refers to Nō robes decorated through that technique.

NUIKIRI: Also called *hira-nui*. An embroidery technique in which comparatively small-sized motifs are freely rendered in satin stitch regardless of the warp and weft structure of the weave. This is the most common technique for depicting a flat surface.

NUI-SHIBORI: Simple-stitch *shibori*. The outlines of the underdrawings are sewn and the threads pulled tightly. Then the fabric is dyed by immersion. Used in linear motifs.

RESIST: Method of preventing dye from penetrating fabric. Resist by sewing and tying is called *shibori* resist and resist by wax, or batik, is called *roketsu*. Paste resist is used mostly in *yūzen* dyeing.

SASHI-NUI: Long-and-short stitch. The inside of a motif is divided into several areas, which are then stitched from the outlines of each area toward the center of the motif in alternating long and short stitches. Used in realistic depictions or for a projected effect such as animal hair, and petals.

SHIBORI: A method of resist dyeing in which the design is reserved by compressing part of the cloth and securing it against dye penetration before immersion dyeing. *See* BŌSHI-SHIBORI, KANOKO-SHIBORI, NUI-SHIBORI.

SHINSEN: Technique of immersing the fabric in the dye, often referred to as immersion dyeing. Used in *shibori* dyeing.

SOMEWAKE: Literally, "divided by dyeing." A type of *kosode* design in which a parti-colored background is created by *shibori* resist techniques, then further decorated with *nuihaku*.

SURIHAKU: Metallic leaf. Paste is applied to the fabric, and gold and/or silver leaf is pressed on. After the paste has dried, the excess leaf is rubbed off to articulate a motif.

TSUJIGAHANA: A combination of surface decorative techniques and the resulting fabrics, which flourished from the sixteenth through early seventeenth centuries. Techniques included are: *shibori*, embroidery, freehand painting, and *surihaku*.

WARI-NUI: A variation of *hira-nui* (satin stitch). The bilaterally symmetrical motif is divided into two areas by its axis and embroidered from its outlines toward the axis. It produces a V shape and is suitable for such motifs as leaves and feathers.

YŪZEN: A combination of techniques using resist paste to define different-colored pattern areas, to create fine white outlines, and to protect pattern areas from the background color, which is usually applied by brush (*hiki-zome*).

Types of Kosode

FURISODE: *Kosode* with elongated sleeves. The seam joining the sleeves to the shoulders is shortened to widen the side hole. Young men and women who were not yet given the adulthood ceremony of *Genbuku* wore this. The length of the sleeve was not regular, and it became longer and longer from the early to mid-Edo period. During the Horeki years (1751–1764) it reached even 2 *shaku*, 8–9 *sun* long (about 60 centimeters long).

HITOE: An unlined garment. With reference to *kosode*, denotes unlined silk or cotton *kosode*.

KATABIRA: Unlined summer *kosode* of various materials other than silk, usually hemp or ramie.

KOSODE: The principal outer garment for all classes since the sixteenth century. It was the precursor of the kimono and similar in cut and proportion. Both sexes wore the *kosode*. The word *kosode* (literally, "small sleeves") refers to the relatively small opening at the wrist, not to the width or length of the sleeve itself. So called to distinguish it from the *ōsode* (large sleeves), worn at the imperial court since Heian times, in which the wrist opening equals the length of the sleeve.

KOSHIMAKI: Literally, "waist wrap." A heavily embroidered *kosode* worn off the shoulders and held at the waist by a sash. It was usually worn over a *katabira* by women of the military elite on formal occasions.

OKUMI: Overlapping sections of half width which are sewn to the edge of the front sections of the *kosode*, making easier the crossing of the front sections.

TAMOTO: Originally referred to the sleeve opening. Where

kosode are concerned, it refers to the hanging bag-style sleeve.

TARIKUBI: Neckbands diagonally crossed in the front, as with *kimono*. Used in comparison with other types of collars such as the *agekubi* (round neck) collar of the *hō* jacket and *kariginu* dress.

UCHIKAKE: A formal outer garment for cool weather, worn unbelted over the *kosode*.

Diagram of a Kosode

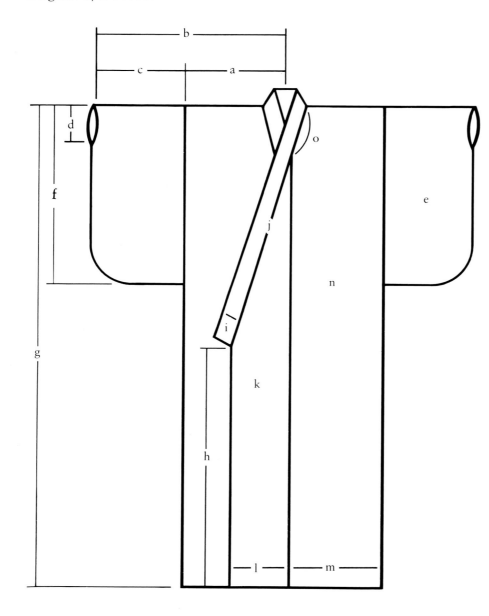

a) *ushiro-haba*: back half-width at hem

b) *yuki*: width between center back to sleeve opening

c) *sode-haba*: sleeve width

d) *sode-guchi*: sleeve opening

e) *sode*: sleeve

f) *sode take*: sleeve length

g) *mi-take*: height

h) *tatezuma*: lower edge of neckband to lower edge of overlap

i) *eri-haba*: neckband width

j) *eri*: neckband

k) *okumi*: overlap

l) *okumi-haba*: overlap width at hem

m) *mae-haba*: front half-width at hem

n) *migoro*: body

o) *okumi-sagari*: top of overlap to shoulder